MAKE YOUR MIND STRONG

Mind Cali Publishing, 2024

MindCali.com

ISBN: 978-1-3999-7629-9

Cover and interior design by Nuno Moreira, NM DESIGN

Mind Callisthenics

MAKE YOUR MIND STRONG

Francis Yates

Contents

Introduction

While we are instinctively drawn to enhancing our physical wellbeing through sports and strength training activities, we often overlook the importance of actively cultivating the strength of our mind with the same vigour.

Our minds can be exercised to become stronger in the same way our muscles respond to training. Exercising our minds establishes new connections and neural pathways; this is possible because of neural plasticity, which gives us the ability to enhance our minds and make them stronger and healthier.

We mostly all want a healthy and strong body; however, we often fall short of our intentions and are good at making excuses for not exercising or eating healthily. Unfortunately, this can result in us waiting for symptoms of problems before taking steps to actively improve our health and strength. This neglect of the preventative benefits we know a strong, healthy body provides can also be seen in our healthcare system. Most of the awareness, time and investment in the healthcare industry is directed to dealing with the symptoms of illness, and understandably preventative healthcare will likely always be less profitable. Preventative healthcare for the body seeks to reduce the likelihood of needing treatments and medicines through the effects of good physical health and strength. *Mind Callisthenics* provides preventative healthcare for your mind.

Body callisthenics, derived from the Greek words *kallos* (beautiful) and *sthenos* (strength), involves performing a variety of bodyweight exercises that exclusively rely on one's own weight to develop muscular strength, improve functional movement patterns and enhance overall physical resilience, without the need for external equipment.

Mind Callisthenics applies these physical callisthenics concepts to your mind. As with physical callisthenics, mind callisthenics is no one-size-fits-all fitness regimen; different elements of our minds require different exercises, and this varies by individual. However, what is consistent for all of us is that exercising our minds requires effort, in the same way we feel the strain when doing press-ups, for example. We each have full autonomy to choose whether we want a weak mind or, in the same way that we can choose to improve our physical health and fitness, we can use exercises to strengthen our minds.

Mind Callisthenics deliberately only provides a functional perspective, focused on practical mind strengthening guidance and exercises; it does not dissect the many layers below the concepts covered. In this sense you should consider it as similar to a user guide for a smartphone or to a cookbook, because it is not intended to explore the technical coding in the microchips or the cellular structure of the ingredients. Practising mind callisthenics is suitable for all ages; we can all enjoy the benefits of exercising our minds, building mind strength and relishing the optimal life experiences and real freedom it enables.

CORE CONCEPTS

The core concepts of mind callisthenics are centred around the idea that much of our modern world is fundamentally different from that of our ancestors, but our minds have changed little. For example:

- We are not fully equipped to deal with the deluge of information in which our modern technology immerses us.
- We have inherited a tendency for fear from our ancestors and, if not

managed, it can manifest in anxiety or depression.

- We are extremely adaptable, which can cause us to quickly take things for granted, from basics to luxuries.

Our minds still work in ways that were once crucial for our ancestors' survival, but in this modern world, some of these ways of working are not as useful any more. In fact, some of the ways our minds work can lead us to make bad choices, decisions and actions, resulting in negative outcomes for us as individuals or as groups.

These potential shortcomings in the way our minds work are similar to the weaknesses in our physical bodies. For example, our craving for fats or sugars is now known to be dangerous for our health if it leads to over-consumption, but was likely crucial for our ancestors' survival. These 'hangovers' we have inherited from our ancestors are like tools in our toolbox that no longer work as well, and carrying the tools around without understanding and managing them creates a risk of harm, like a broken hammer or, even worse, a leaking blowtorch.

We know our physical bodies are predisposed to these types of weaknesses, and we undertake nutritional interventions and challenging physical exercises to control them. In the same way, mind callisthenics helps us do this for our minds by providing insight into potential weaknesses, so we can actively monitor them and build mind strength to manage and control them. These potential weaknesses are like 'comfort foods', which feel good but can become extremely unhealthy. Examples include:

- our deep desire to join groups, teams or tribes
- irresistible shortcuts that create errors in our interpretation of information, including biases, assumptions, inferences and expectations
- our discomfort with the unknown
- our tendency and preference for quick decision-making at the expense of substance and nuance

- how we notice only a limited number of things in front of us; our attention is selective and narrow
- our aversion to holding two competing ideas in our minds, our instinct being to rapidly accept one and disregard the other
- relentlessly seeking out patterns, even where they do not exist

Developing an awareness of, and techniques to manage, these tendencies is important for both our mind health and strength. This is especially true in our modern world, which is characterised by rapidly accelerating change combined with an almost overwhelming information flow. Understanding our potential weaknesses and instead turning them into strengths by exercising our minds is something we all can and should be doing, in the same way we go to the gym, eat a balanced diet or even brush our teeth.

BROADER CONCEPTS

Around the core concepts are broader concepts, where we explore how our modern world contrasts with that of our ancestors. Understanding this contrast helps us explore how our minds are working in this modern world context.

Figure 1 illustrates simplistically how knowledge is created in our minds and, in particular, the importance of information in this knowledge creation process. 'Information flow' is described as the process of external information entering our minds through our five senses, with the majority of information tending to be visual or auditory, and increasingly, in our modern world, through digital technology devices.

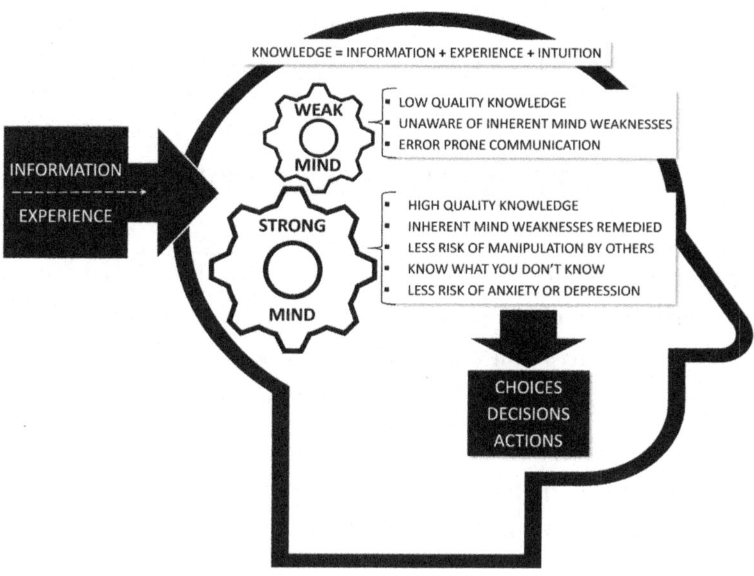

FIGURE 1

There is no doubt that the information flow in the modern world would be completely unrecognisable to our ancestors, but our minds are essentially the same. We explore the gap between what we have and what is optimal in our modern world and consider solutions to overcome this gap. Importantly, this involves developing an understanding of our personal information flow and how we use it to receive information into our minds, including the various ways in which the information flow and our communication are imperfect. We explore how we can effectively identify, interpret and challenge these imperfections, and then actively filter and control them, so we are consistently building high-quality knowledge and making optimal decisions, choices and actions.

Another important concept explored is our awareness of overall mind health and how to improve it, together with a deeper understanding of how we relate to the wider world, both through our individual relationships and as part of a global population of over 8 billion minds.

HOW TO USE MIND CALLISTHENICS

Our minds are similar to a muscle in the sense that the more we exercise them, the stronger they become. Mind callisthenics is a set of tools that provide exercises for our minds. The process of thinking through, digesting and challenging the concepts and the exercises in each chapter, strengthens our minds. Like physical callisthenics exercises, we don't need lots of equipment, and primarily use our own bodies to build physical strength. With mind callisthenics, we are building strength using our own minds.

A significant amount of our mind activity happens automatically in our subconscious. While we cannot directly control this, we can influence and shape our subconscious through what we do with our conscious mind. We can do this in the moment, through active awareness and iterative interventions, and also over the medium and long term, through more consistent practice and habit forming. Ultimately, the most effective way to influence our subconscious is to resonate with its main motivators; these are the drive for happiness and avoidance of suffering, and fight or flight in the more extreme short term.

Monitoring and awareness of what our subconscious does and how it does it provides us with clarity on the things it does well and where it has weaknesses. This self-awareness provides us with the opportunity to make interventions using the conscious elements of our minds to ensure we are arriving at optimal outcomes; this is a crucial element of mind strengthening. As we reinforce these interventions – for example, by performing the exercises – they permeate back into our subconscious as part of an iterative improvement and strengthening of our minds.

EXERCISING OUR MINDS

Each chapter concludes with exercises that enable you to build your mind strength in relation to the topics covered. Actively thinking and wrestling with the key concepts and pathway-triggering questions will develop and boost your neural pathways and cognitive capability, and will even enable you to self-identify areas for further development. The outcome is very similar to exercising your muscles; that is, your noticeably stronger muscles and your stronger mind.

While thinking through the exercises, consider writing or drawing, known as sensorimotor engagement. The coordination of sensory and motor systems, together with the tactile feedback of a pen, can enhance your cognitive processing.

Another a useful approach when exercising your mind is 'see one, do one, teach one'. This three-step model is a well-established and proven technique to build neural pathways. While the technique was developed for learning surgical techniques, the concept applies just as well to any domain and is an exceptionally reliable way to enhance our minds' capacity and capabilities.

Finally, making analogies and using metaphors is a very effective technique to build neural pathways. It is particularly powerful since it requires us to forge connections between unrelated ideas or concepts, often through lateral thought processes. Whether we are creating our own analogies and metaphors or exploring those that already exist, it is great exercise for your mind. The activity challenges us to get to the key element or concept, while we try to map on to a different context. While doing this it can feel like we are 'stretching' our minds, which is often an indication we are creating new neural pathways – the mind strength equivalent of muscles. Being forced to think deeply to get to the core of the knowledge or concept, and then trying to map this on to a different context, is a highly effective and satisfying mind exercise technique.

You can build the exercises into a regular routine covering the range of topics on a rolling basis, or pick up a specific area of focus, for example, if you are triggered by an event in your life. The exercises can be revisited as often as you like and can be performed in any order. Investing time and effort to perform each exercise deeply will provide significantly better mind strengthening results, but will inevitably be tiring. As with physical exercises, be careful not to overtrain, space out your exercise sessions and ensure you give yourself appropriate recovery time, recognising the insights covered in Chapter 6, Optimising Overall Mind Health. Determining how to perform the exercises most effectively will depend on you, so whether it is actively thinking and wrestling with the key concepts, using pathway-triggering questions, sensorimotor engagement, 'see one, do one, teach one', creating analogies or metaphors or something else, embrace what works best for you as you travel the journey to a strong mind. To borrow a quote from cycling[1]: the road never gets easier, you just get stronger.

THE JOURNEY AHEAD

1. Modern World, Old Brains

The context in which our brains operate has changed drastically over the last 20 years, and this rate of change is significantly higher than during any other period of human history. This chapter explores the challenges these changes have created, and continue to create, and how you can be aware, adapt and navigate them effectively.

2. Core Mind Strength

This chapter explores the core components of mind strength, helping us understand how elements of our mind work and providing insight into potential weaknesses. This is similar to having a basic understanding of how key parts of our bodies work, which we might learn in school. There are also practical suggestions for improvement through mind exercises.

3. Building Your Foundation

Building a strong mind requires a solid foundation, and the most fundamental concept in our foundation is knowledge. This chapter helps with our understanding of how knowledge is created and operates in our minds. We also explore the concept that there are different levels of certainty for each of the elements of knowledge in our minds, and why that is important.

4. Tuning Your Mind's Ear

This chapter helps you build awareness of the many types of issues that can exist with the deluge of information flowing into our minds in the context of our modern world. We explore how we filter, interpret and process information flow, why this creates challenges, and solutions to address these challenges.

5. The Problem With Words

Transferring the vast complexity of some knowledge or meaning, unique to your mind's network of neurons and synapses, into someone else's mind, is subject to significant noise and interference. We tend to think of words as conveying meaning with the precision of a fine paintbrush, but in practice, they can be more similar to throwing an open tin of paint. This chapter helps us understand what can potentially go wrong with our communication and how we can mitigate these issues.

6. Optimising Overall Mind Health

The focus of this book is on mind strength; however, without a good level of mind health, your mind strength is almost irrelevant. This chapter explores factors that contribute to mind health and how you can strive to maintain them at an optimal level. We know the health of our bodies is at the foundation of any strength we have in our muscles and bones, and this is the same for strength in our minds.

7. Who Are the Other 8 Billion People?

The focus of this chapter is understanding why we tend to obsessively focus on our differences, given our minds are overwhelmingly more similar than different to one another's. We explore how this tendency skews the reality we perceive, and the wonderful benefits, and some downsides, of empathy in helping us navigate these challenges.

Chapter 1.
Modern World, Old Brains

Over the past 200 years, the context in which our brains operate has changed radically, with the most pervasive changes occurring in the last 20 years. This period has witnessed an unprecedented surge in the proliferation and accessibility of vast volumes of information, with rapid technological innovation influencing every aspect of our lives and fundamental changes in our global interpersonal experiences across our 8 billion plus minds. Despite these changes, our minds remain utterly extraordinary in their power and complexity. However, the modern context has introduced some new challenges that we need to be aware of, adapt to and navigate effectively.

These challenges stem from inherited features of our minds that were crucial for our ancestors' survival but can become weaknesses in our modern context. If we are not aware of these weaknesses and do not control them, this can cause us to make decisions, choices or actions that are suboptimal or even dangerous for our survival.

INFORMATION FLOW

Our brains are optimal for working in the environment of our ancestors; however, they now operate in a different context. Modern technology means that our senses are constantly overwhelmed with an unlimited information flow through multiple sources concurrently. We are essentially in an 'experiment' where our minds are being tested to survive a limitless deluge of information. This deluge has been increasing, and continues to increase, exponentially, and yet we still have minimal personal or governmental regulation of the information flow. This 'experiment' on the human mind is not a deliberate act; we have collectively created it by accident through many well-intentioned technological innovations, but we are nonetheless going to have to live with the consequences. We are observing the results in real time, similar to the proliferation of cigarettes in the early 20th century.

Understanding this context is crucial because information is so important to our minds – it is an essential component that, together with experience and intuition, enables us to create knowledge in our minds. However, the current 'experiment' presents significant challenges to the information flow arriving in our minds. We need to be aware of these challenges so we can proactively manage how we digest the information flow; this includes awareness of the following types of problematic information flow:

- Information flow that only exists for its own sake; some information flow only exists to be consumed, and this is the sender's only incentive. The quality or veracity of the actual information is completely irrelevant to the sender, whose only motive is that we consume the information. The dynamics of the advertising industry largely contribute to this phenomenon. For example, on social media or 24-hour news channels, the primary objective is to keep people hooked; the consumers are, in fact, the commodity. The focus is on maximising audience size to boost advertising revenue, with little regard for the quality or relevance of the information provided as long as ensures the maximum possible level of consumption.

- Information flow that is intended and designed to motivate a specific response (emotional or rational), usually to support the information sender's agenda, whether that is commercial, political or otherwise. This information flow can be specifically targeted at the people the sender is seeking to influence, with the veracity or accuracy of the information being irrelevant. The information and interpretations contained in this information flow are often manipulated. An example would be political or activist misinformation to influence elections or public opinion.

Awareness of these features of information flow is important to help us build mind strength and, ultimately, navigate these challenges. In addition to awareness, we can actively challenge the information flow by not taking information at face value and asking:

- Where is this information flow coming from?
- How is the sender incentivised to invest time and resources in creating this information flow?
- What does that incentivisation mean about the motivation, quality or veracity of this information?
- How can I corroborate this information?
- Does this information feel like it is too good to be true?
- Does it induce an emotional response?
- Particularly where an emotional response is induced, do you find yourself inclined to 'take a side' and overlook a lack data that supports the assertions?
- Consider if there is balance within the information – are there are different points of view presented? Are there any counterarguments to the main information or analysis presented? If only one side of an argument is presented, why is that?

By being aware and actively challenging the information flow, we are likely to improve the quality of information we digest, which means:

- We can validate the knowledge we have or be considered and careful as we create knowledge in our minds (in Chapter 3: Building Your Foundation, we explore how we create knowledge in our minds).
- We can dispel misinformation or myths.
- We can discover and investigate new truths.
- Ultimately, we can make better-informed decisions, choices and actions.

In Chapter 4: Tuning Your Mind's Ear, we explore tools and techniques we can use to regulate the quality and veracity of the information flowing into our minds. This includes exploring how we filter, interpret and process the information flow and how awareness of the challenges with the information flow and active interventions can help ensure our choices, decisions and actions are based on high-quality knowledge and clear insight into our level of certainty.

PROGRAMMED FOR FEAR

Our minds have a natural tendency for fear. This is not to say we spend all our time, or indeed any of our time, in abject fear. However, by exploring the factors at work, we can be aware of and manage our innate fear tendencies. Fear has been crucial for our survival, serving as a protective mechanism and alerting us to potential threats or dangers in our environment. Our ancestors were often subjected to a huge range of threats; by being instinctively fearful and quickly anticipating and responding to threats, they were able to survive. However, this predisposition is not as useful in our modern world. Today, we are subject to far fewer threats to our survival, but our minds, with the same neural circuitry and neurotransmitters, have the same tendency for fear. In essence, while the nature and significance of the threats we face today are different, we still have the same fear responses of our ancestors.

The charts in Figure 2 below roughly illustrate the concept that while we face the same challenges as our ancestors, the necessary levels of worry and fear required in the modern world are comparatively lower. This can result in our minds having a disproportionate level of fear and worry about areas that are not as important as the level of fear and worry we ascribe to them.

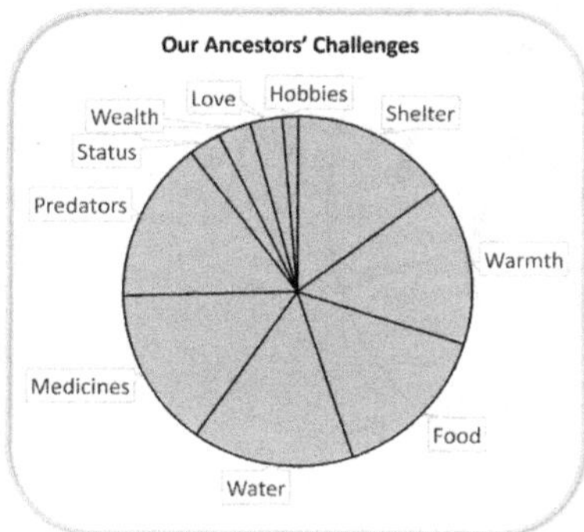

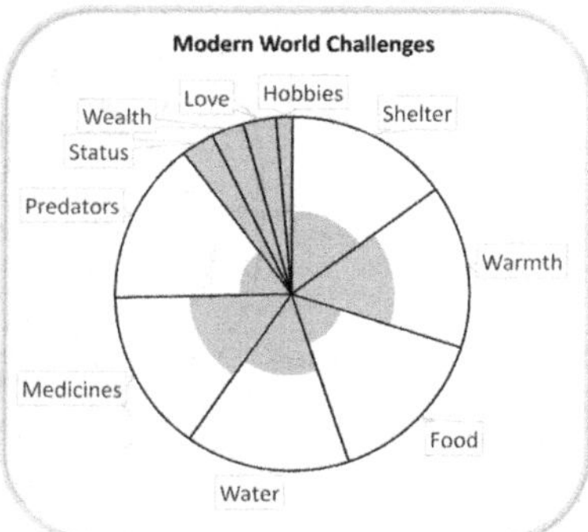

FIGURE 2

The identical size of the circles is representative of our minds in the modern world having the same capacity and capability for fear and worry as those of our ancestors. However, the actual required extent of our fear and worry about challenges has, on the whole, reduced, meaning we have an 'excess' of fear and worry. This 'excess' fear and worry is inherent in our minds and is a result of our context changing more quickly than our minds have changed in their propensity for fear. If we do not manage this misalignment – or worse, if we are not aware of it – it is likely to drive a disproportionate level of fear and worry into challenges that do not warrant it, such as status or wealth. These disproportionate levels of fear or worry are likely to manifest as stress and anxiety. Figure 3 illustrates this concept, with the white areas being subsumed into the grey areas, representative of our fear and worry finding new homes in challenges that likely do not warrant them.

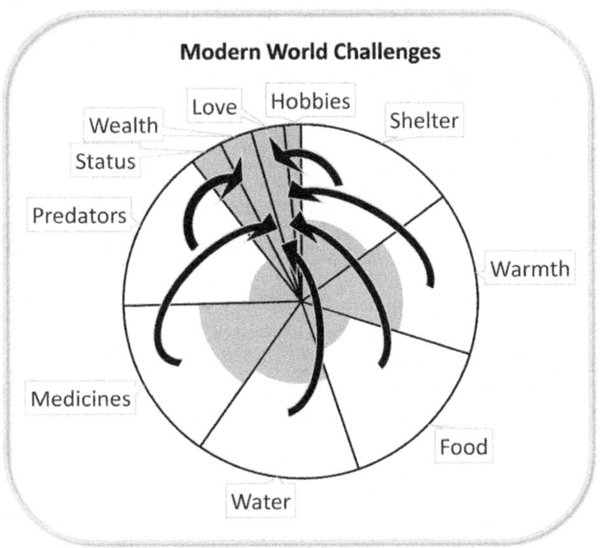

FIGURE 3

In summary, our propensity for fear or worry is the same as that of our ancestors. However, the extent to which we actually need to worry about things has reduced, and this results in us having an excess of fear and worry. It is similar to a race car driver revving the engine before the start of the race, causing the engine to overheat before the race starts, or a racehorse stuck in a small paddock, pacing back and forth with no opportunity to run free. Recognising and being self-aware of this feature of our minds is crucial, as it enables us to manage our responses to ensure they are proportionate to our modern world context.

A good example of this proportionality is considering that your fight-or-flight response to being chased by a predator in a jungle should be significantly higher than your response to social, relationship, financial or work worries. Challenge yourself: do you really have a completely different level of stress response, and if it is in any way similar, consider how you can moderate your non-jungle response by considering it through this relative perspective.

If we do not actively monitor and seek to control our stress response, it can often lead to chronic stress. We know that overexposure to stress hormones has negative effects on the body, including impaired immune function, increased risk of chronic disease and mind health problems. These hormones include cortisol, adrenaline and noradrenaline, which are released by the adrenal gland and increase our heart rate, blood pressure and respiration rate to prepare our body for action. However, this level of action is generally not needed in our modern lives, and repeated overexposure to these effects manifests as mind and physical health issues.

TOO ADAPTABLE

Humans are phenomenally adaptable; we quickly comprehend our environment and specific context and immediately seek to thrive further. Fundamental to this ability is an intrinsic drive to not be content. Our minds are constantly striving for more, and this is what has made us so successful in surviving and thriving. This drive to not be content is the fundamental reason we exist as we do now, and without it, we would not have been able to, and would not continue to, innovate and constantly improve. Our ancestors had this drive, and their peers who did not have this drive effectively ended their days in their caves. However, within a modern context, this drive is not always helpful.

The same level of 'lack of contentment' exists in our minds as in our ancestors' minds. However, the usefulness of this level of lack of contentment has changed. In our modern world, safety, warmth, healthcare and food are accessible for many, but the lack of contentment level in our minds remains the same. We rapidly take our environment for granted, and as soon as we have something, we want more. This is not our fault but is, in fact, intrinsic to our minds. To ensure it does not have any adverse impacts (e.g. anxiety or depression), we need to alter our perspectives.

If we are actively aware of recognising when our minds have an unjustified lack of contentment, we can challenge the effect this has on our perspective or understanding of our environment and specific context.

One way to challenge the effect of a lack of contentment on our perspective is to practise gratitude for the good things in our lives and actively feel thankful for them, we explore this in further detail in the Chapter 6 section Practising Gratitude and Generosity. Feeling thankful for the good things in our lives sounds simple, however even when done regularly, over time our inherent tendency is for this to become increasingly superficial. This tendency away from a deep gratitude and to an increase in taking things for granted, is driven by the power of our lack of contentment. However, when we are able to overcome this superficiality, practising gratitude has powerful effects on our mind health, such as increased happiness, improved relationships and less risk of depression and anxiety. Deliberately skewing our focus to aspects of our lives we are grateful for helps us shift our perspectives away from negative thinking patterns, which tend to fuel feelings of stress and unhappiness. Our intentional focus on what we are thankful for helps cultivate our sense of positivity and contentment and, therefore, addresses the inherent downside of our minds being so phenomenally adaptable. Further techniques to help take control of our perspective are covered in Chapter 2 in the sections on control and perspectives.

TECHNOLOGY TROUBLES

Our minds' weaknesses with respect to information flow (being programmed for fear or being too adaptable) are all amplified and exacerbated by modern technology. The proliferation and deep penetration of modern technology into virtually all elements of our lives has resulted in some new side effects. These are particularly acute in younger generations, whose formative minds have been fully immersed from a young, impressionable age. Research from the Dove Self-Esteem Project, involving over 7,500 individuals, revealed that 80% of young people perceived their peers to be addicted to social media. Additionally, 50% of the surveyed youth expressed that social media induced anxiety among themselves and their friends[2]. The full impact of this immersion, including on body image,[3] bullying and suicide,[4] is not yet known; while some effects may be benign, it is clear there have already been significant detrimental impacts to both individuals and society as a whole.

NORMALISATION OF IMMEDIACY

The proliferation of technology has driven the normalisation of immediacy and has resulted in a cultural shift towards instant gratification. We now expect goods to be delivered within hours or even minutes and services to be available at a moment's notice. Our minds increasingly want immediate answers to questions, and we seek immediate entertainment and stimulation. The erosion of our ability to be patient has made waiting for anything, even for a few seconds, a stressful experience. We now crave instant validation and feedback through technology.

However, this normalisation of immediacy in our minds has significant detrimental side effects, including increased stress and anxiety as our patience is tested, decreased social connections as we spend significant amounts of our time in a virtual world and a significant decrease in our ability to be present in and enjoy the moment because of our impatience for the next thing.

Patience is an extremely valuable element in our minds. It allows us to delay gratification and persevere through difficulties, which ultimately leads to greater success, satisfaction, and fulfilment in the long run. There are no shortcuts for these experiences. When we exercise patience, we also have a greater capacity to plan, create strategies and make better decisions, which will often lead to better outcomes. The simple act of waiting can build anticipation and excitement, which leads to greater enjoyment and appreciation when we finally receive what we have been waiting for. The cultivation of patience can also increase our capacity for empathy because we have more time to consider all sides of a situation, and we have the time and patience to engage in substantive conversation and develop meaningful relationships.

ELIMINATION OF REAL HUMAN CONTACT

The significant advancement of technology over the last 20 years has led to the rapid elimination of real human contact as virtual interactions increasingly replace face-to-face communication. This manifests in various ways, such as the preference for texting and emailing instead of phone or in-person conversations, the use of technology to form personal relationships and the automation of customer service and support. It is indisputable that technology has significantly increased the ease of communicating across distances; however, at the same time it has created a barrier to genuine human connection, leading to increased loneliness, isolation and social disconnection for many.

Using technology as your sole source of communication can lead to misunderstandings and miscommunications as non-verbal cues and tone of voice are lost. Our minds also lose the significant health benefits of the chemicals that are released during real-world interactions. To keep our minds healthy and strong, we should ensure we are aware, actively manage a balance between using technology, seek face-to-face communication and limit 'screen time'.

BALANCE BETWEEN REAL-LIFE EXPERIENCE AND OUR TECHNOLOGY LIVES

Our minds face a significant challenge in finding a balance between real life and our technology lives. Our technology lives are a recent phenomenon and extremely powerful, with many of us feeling the version of ourselves created in technology systems is a real person. We also regularly see other people's technology versions of themselves as real people. Clearly, this is not the case; while the illusion is powerful and enjoyable to revel in, as with any dopamine reward-triggering system, balanced usage is crucial. While we know about the importance of balance in terms of things like gambling and drugs, we are in general behind the curve in catching up to the addictive powers and consequences of modern technology. The collateral damage from getting this balance wrong is our real lives, real relationships and real minds.

Modern technology has provided, and continues to provide, many benefits, most notably increased productivity and efficiency. However, with no limits or control on proliferation and penetration, this imbalance is increasingly driving many negative consequences, particularly for children, such as addiction, distraction and disconnection from the natural world. These negative consequences then cause further knock-on effects, such as reduced productivity, decreased creativity and negative impacts on mind health and wellbeing.

We should use our minds to control this imbalance through active prioritisation of self-awareness and intentionality of technology use. We can do this by setting boundaries, such as limiting our time and intensity of technology use and ensuring we prioritise time spent in nature, creative pursuits and meaningful human connections. Establishing boundaries will help with achieving an optimal balance, allowing our minds to embrace the benefits of technology while remaining grounded in the real world.

DOPAMINE NUMBING

Dopamine has an important role in how our mind functions with respect to motivation, reward and pleasure. Dopamine is a neurotransmitter; these are the chemicals used to pass signals between neurons via synapses. We typically have over a hundred billion neurons and this 'neural network' of neurons and synapses is responsible for transmitting and processing information in our brains. A useful analogy to help understanding could be a jazz duet of a piano and saxophone, where the musicians communicate with each other through their respective instruments via sound waves; neurotransmitters are the sound waves in this analogy, with neurons taking the role of the musicians. We explore neurotransmitters further in Chapter 6.

The proliferation of technology, and digital communications in particular, into many aspects of our personal and working lives has driven and accelerated our minds to become increasingly numb, and addicted, to dopamine. The rewards we perceive when we use technology trigger a relatively strong (given the effort involved) release of dopamine, which provides feelings of pleasure. However, as these feelings of pleasure fade, we crave more dopamine, and are able to satisfy this demand instantly through the continued use of the technology. This cycle reinforces the behaviour and ultimately provides the structure for forming an addiction.

The dopamine reward system was essential for our ancestors, motivating them to engage in activities that would have helped their surviving and thriving, such as eating, sex, social interactions and, importantly, the anticipation of these activities. However, with this new technology, perceived rewards – for example 'likes', which are perceived as social validation – trigger more frequent, sustained and often higher-intensity dopamine release relative to that which triggered our traditional surviving and thriving activities. This reward system 'hack' causes a desensitisation of our minds to the effects of dopamine; while it is not fully understood how the hack works, it seems to be driven by:

- negligible effort and 'low-cost' dopamine release relative to the traditional surviving and thriving dopamine triggers inherited from our ancestors
- constant and immediate stimulation, allowing for continuous consumption, with information available whenever you want it
- high-intensity stimulation triggered by visual and aural excitement
- expectation conditioning, where anticipation of reward can have as powerful a dopamine effect as the actual reward (this is similar to the placebo effect, which is explored in Chapter 2)
- harnessing our hard-wired reward stimulators, such as eating, sex,

and social interactions, and then super-charging them using all the points listed above

This dopamine desensitisation means that when we are not using this technology, we need more stimulation to experience the same level of motivation, reward and pleasure. Unfortunately, this reduction in stimulation impact affects those stimulations that tend to be healthier and have a lesser reinforcement cycle, and are therefore less likely to be addictive.

The downsides of this dopamine numbing and increasing addiction to technology are numerous and have both short- and long-term implications. In the short term, dopamine numbing can lead to decreased motivation and difficulty concentrating. This can impact our ability to perform in daily life, leading to decreased productivity and difficulties in maintaining relationships. In the long term, dopamine numbing can lead to a decrease in overall life satisfaction as the ability to experience pleasure and reward is diminished, resulting in a likely increase of symptoms such as depression and anxiety.

Ultimately, as with all addictive behaviours, people will seek out more and more stimulation to achieve the same level of pleasure and reward. At the same time, they require their 'fix' just to get through the day. We see this increasingly with social media, and particularly with infinity scrolling, which never seems to scratch that itch.

Since the technology causing dopamine numbing is relatively new and changing rapidly, we have not yet started to control it properly and, as a result, our minds are particularly vulnerable. The risk is that technology is moving from being a useful tool to becoming a crutch, as we are increasingly reliant on it and forming addictive behaviours.

We can hope that in 10 or 20 years, there will be regulation and control to mitigate these damaging effects. However, in the meantime, we can seek to protect our minds by limiting, and balancing our exposure to technology and instead engaging in activities that release dopamine in a more balanced way, such as exercise, spending time in nature and connecting with others in person.

FAKE IT UNTIL YOU MAKE IT

In our modern world, there is an overwhelming focus on 'optics' or appearance at the expense of substance. This is causing us to be content with, and even satisfied by, superficial, surface-level knowledge and understanding. Technology, and digital communications in particular, amplify this effect. Increasingly, we consider surface-level conclusions developed by others as sufficient without delving deeper into the underlying components that shape that understanding. Without understanding the building blocks, we are vulnerable to absorbing distorted knowledge and even complete falsehoods, and risk being manipulated by others as a result.

Virtue signalling is increasingly prevalent and is driven by this contentment with the superficial. Virtue signalling describes an intent to demonstrate our own righteousness, or moral superiority, through expressing opinions or taking part in activities that align with social or political values to gain the attention and approval of others. When the virtue that is being signalled is based on and amplified through digital communications, it has a particularly pernicious impact on distorting information flow and degrading our collective knowledge and ability to solve problems and improve our societies. We can see this with the projection of opinions purely based on them being the opposite of what is perceived as morally deficient. Unfortunately, this in itself is rarely sufficient for the opinion to have any veracity, despite the feeling that it does and the virtue that is signalled. It is entirely possible for opposing opinions to both lack any moral or rational substance.

The increasing contentment with superficial or surface-level knowledge and understanding is also making our minds brittle. Increasingly, any challenge or enquiry into surface knowledge, concepts or meaning is perceived as a criticism rather than normal discourse. This perception of criticism and offence limits our ability to develop our minds, since we are unable to build our own knowledge, concepts or meaning effectively, and restricted in our ability to learn anything from others.

A further side effect of this trend of form over substance is that it limits our ability to share and discuss nuance. This is problematic because nuance is so crucial to understanding knowledge and concepts, and the importance increases in relation to the complexity of the knowledge or concepts being discussed. Increasingly, we are becoming uninterested in any nuance because of a tendency to seek shortcuts, normalise immediacy or virtue signal. Ultimately, this trend will slow our ability to progress our collective knowledge and will act as a drag on our development as a global population.

TRADITIONAL MIND CAPABILITIES WE ARE LOSING

Modern technology is so powerful that it has become a crutch for our minds and is causing us to start to lose capabilities passed down from our ancestors. Some of the most salient examples today include:

- navigating the physical world, including our sense of direction and our ability to create or visualise routes between geographical points in our minds

- performing mental arithmetic – and even if we do perform it, we have little confidence in our outputs
- being 'in the moment' and taking in the full experience – instead choosing to prioritise capturing it on photos or videos for supposedly enjoying at another time
- the ability to recall events without the aid of photos or videos – excessive reliance on the crutch of technology
- problem-solving and critical thinking
- innovating, particularly when it relates to creating something from nothing
- taking the initiative – being proactive versus passively receiving instructions
- persevering and understanding the value of patience, with an appreciation of 'journey versus destination'
- active listening, basic face-to-face interpersonal skills and our ability to read body language

In addition to these lost capabilities, we are experiencing a generally diminished curiosity and a sense of futility because of the enormous power of technology as an information source. Increasingly, there is an illusion developing in our minds that everything has already been discovered and all answers are already available through our digital communications technology. This is causing a withering and loss of the fundamental skills that enable us to critique, offer an original perspective or challenge, when actually these skills are critically important in our modern world.

GENERATIVE ARTIFICIAL INTELLIGENCE

Recent paradigm-changing advances in generative artificial intelligence (Gen AI) provide excellent tools to help with mind callisthenics exercises.

This is because they provide significant improvement in our access to information in regard to nuance and understanding multiple sources. More nuanced information and a wider range of evidence are hugely beneficial as enablers for critical thinking and help us interpret our information flow.

Gen AI should also enable a more transparent flagging of information for reliability and veracity, such as identification of where there may be biases, assumptions, inferences or expectations. There is also a likelihood of more tailoring of information specifically for you; this reduces the effect of noise or distortion. For example, an information flow tailored to your specific intelligence type or personality traits could help that information resonate more strongly with you.

However, as well as these significant upsides of Gen AI, there are potentially more downsides. The amount of processing power that we can now outsource from our minds means we will certainly be exercising our minds less in certain areas than we currently are. It is important to ensure we continue exercising in different ways to maintain our mind strength. We need to deliberately seek to identify what mind strengths we value and how we want to retain and maintain those strengths rather than letting them wither. For example, blindly relying on outputs from Gen AI could lead to us losing the ability to even know how to validate the outputs or challenge them altogether.

EXERCISES

Exercise your mind by actively thinking through and wrestling with the key concept: that the minds we have inherited from our ancestors have some potential pitfalls in our modern world context. Ponder on the areas discussed and use the questions below to develop and boost your neural pathways. As with exercising your muscles, your mind will become stronger as you exercise it. Experiment with different ways of exercising and see which techniques work best for you:

- Explore in your mind – try it with your eyes closed or while doing physical exercise.
- Write down your thoughts, draw concepts or talk out loud to yourself.
- Work with others in dialogue.

Consider the key concepts below. Do you agree with their premises? If not, why not? And if you do, why do you agree?

- We are essentially in an 'experiment' in our modern world, and this experiment is testing the capacity of our anciently developed brains to survive a limitless deluge of information:

  1. Our brains are not in their optimum environment in this modern world.

  2. Modern technology, and digital communications in particular, is causing our senses to be constantly overwhelmed by an unlimited information flow through multiple sources concurrently.

  3. Our tendency for fear, which served our ancestors well, can manifest as unnecessary anxiety and stress in our modern world.

  4. Our ability to quickly adapt to our environment can result in us unhelpfully taking things for granted, reducing our capacity for gratitude and happiness and increasing the likelihood of anxiety and stress.

- Think about obvious examples of 'information flow existing for its own sake' – that is, where its entire purpose is for us to consume it because the sender of the information is incentivised in some way (clickbait, for example).

  1. Now think about examples with the same features where the information only exists for us to consume, but that is more nuanced with other motives – for example, 24-hour news.

2. Next, apply this logic to other examples and think about them from the perspective of the information sender. How important is the quality or veracity of the information to them compared to their need for you to consume it?

- Think about some examples of information flow designed entirely to motivate a specific response, whether emotional or rational:

  1. Think of examples where you see this happening to others or to yourself, where it is clear that the information is overwhelmingly intended to evoke, or even provoke, a response that is likely aligned to the information sender's agenda, whether that is commercial, political or otherwise.

  2. Put yourself in the shoes of the sender of that information. How important to the sender of that information flow is the quality or veracity of that information compared to their need to influence the receiver?

- Key considerations to understand the quality or veracity of information flow are as follows:

  1. Where is this information flow coming from?

  2. How is the sender incentivised to invest time and resources in creating this information flow?

  3. What does that incentivisation mean about the motivation, quality or veracity of this information?

  4. How can I corroborate this information?

  5. Does this information feel like it is too good to be true?

  6. Does it induce an emotional response?

  7. Particularly where an emotional response is induced, do you find yourself inclined to 'take a side' and overlook a lack of data that supports the assertions?

  8. Are there any counterarguments, information or analysis presented? If only one side of an argument is presented, why is that?

- Think about whether you agree that your propensity to fear or worry is the same as that of your ancestors:

1. Do you agree that the extent to which we need to worry about some things has reduced, and this results in us having an excess of fear and worry?

2. Do you think we are fundamentally different from our ancestors?

3. Put yourself in your ancestors' shoes. Do you think you have any less propensity to be fearful or worried?

- Practise self-awareness when you feel your fight-or-flight response kicking in – that is, the effects of cortisol, adrenaline or noradrenaline increasing your heart rate, blood pressure and respiration rate – and try to relativise your context to that of your ancestors being chased by a predator.

1. Embracing the perspective that, relatively speaking, your situation is less acute, and that you should therefore be less fearful (at least in theory), can be a useful tool to help moderate and temper your fight-or-flight response.

2. Try to be consistently self-aware of this feature of your mind and use relativisation to manage and moderate your response to your context.

- Self-analyse what you take for granted in your life. A simple way to do this is to imagine yourself 500 years ago and compare what you have now to that version of you:

1. Consider the importance of the things you have now compared to what you had 500 years ago.

2. How much do you actively embrace and feel grateful for those things every day?

3. Can you make this gratitude part of a more regular routine or even embed it in your general outlook?

- Think about your ability to be patient:

1. Can you cultivate your patience to allow you to be more in control of the outcome?

2. Can you try to actively enjoy the journey and the moment more, rather than having a myopic obsession with the destination or goal?

3. Practise delaying gratification – for example:
    - not consuming all the cakes, or whatever your vice is, in the packet and instead try and make them last all week.
    - resisting the option to binge-watch a TV series and watch it over several weeks instead.
    - training or exercising every day, even when the results or your desired physical changes are not noticeable.

- Change your perspective so that these challenges are actually opportunities to build your mind's strength and resilience; embrace them in the same way you would hit the gym to work on your weight training to enhance your body's physical endurance.

- Deliberately seek out and immerse yourself in real human contact. Anything from walking in a town square to dancing in a nightclub will decrease loneliness, isolation and social disconnection.

- Do you suspect there are elements of your engagement with modern technology that are not good for you?

    1. Speculate on the regulation that will exist in 10 or 20 years to limit addiction to harmful technology.

    2. Can you think of ways to self-moderate your use of technology now rather than waiting for government regulation?

    3. Consider that smoking regulations took decades to be implemented after research first showed it was harmful.

    4. Think about some of the recent interventions; for example, China is exploring a 40-minute screen time restriction for children under eight years old, the UK has plans to ban all phones in schools and some senior tech leaders in Silicon Valley choose to send their own children to schools with minimal or no technology.

- Consider the effect technology has had on our bodies, reducing our physical activity and driving obesity. How do these effects compare to the impact that it has had on our minds in the last 20 years – do you see any parallels?

- Can you think of examples where technology has effectively become a crutch for your mind?

- Consider some of these examples to reduce your reliance on technology and strengthen your mind:

  1. Navigate the physical world, including your sense of direction and ability to create or visualise routes between geographical points, in your mind.

  2. Perform mental arithmetic.

  3. Actively listen to improve basic face-to-face interpersonal skills and your ability to read body language.

  4. Practise problem-solving and deliberately develop your critical thinking skills.

  5. Innovate, particularly where it relates to creating something from nothing.

  6. Take the initiative by being proactive versus passively receiving instructions.

- Consider where you or others may have fallen into the trap of virtue signalling and what the impact is on your ability to actually reach common ground.

- Can you think of examples where you have been tempted to take an opinion purely because it appears to be the opposite of something you superficially consider to be morally or rationally deficient?

- Challenge yourself – does just taking an opposite opinion mean that is has any veracity?

- Think about how you can use Gen AI to help with determining the reliability and veracity of information:

  1. How can it help with understanding and framing nuance more clearly for you and others?

2. How does it enable you to consult more sources more efficiently?

- Consider how you want to maintain your ability to challenge the outputs of Gen AI:

  1. How can you be sure of the completeness, accuracy or validity of these outputs, and what would you want to validate independently?

  2. How can you make sure you retain the skills to be able to do the activities you are outsourcing to technology from your mind?

  3. What steps do you need to take to maintain your skills and ensure they are not diminished?

Chapter 2.
Core Mind Strength

Our minds are like a muscle – the more we exercise them, the stronger they get. Understanding how your mind functions is important to enable you to effectively exercise and strengthen it. This is similar to the basic understanding of how your body works that's required to improve your physical health and fitness, such as awareness of diet, breathing, circulation, muscles, bones, joints and so on. Take time to think through, digest and challenge the following concepts; while they may seem obvious or extensions of your existing knowledge, collectively they form the core of your mind strength.

YOU HAVE FULL CONTROL

Your brain is the most complex organ in your body. It has an incredible capacity for change due to its neuroplasticity. This essentially means that new neural pathways are created in response to our experiences and our thinking. This plasticity means you have full autonomy and control to develop, build and strengthen any neural pathways in your conscious mind. However, this reality is not always clear to us, as we have a tendency for inertia and a reluctance to actively intervene and challenge or change how our minds are working. By recognising this tendency, we can overcome the inertia and drive change, deliberately create new pathways and increase the strength of our conscious minds.

It is important to also understand that our subconscious mind is responsible for a significant amount of our mind activity. Exactly how our subconscious works remains mysterious; however, we can observe the results as they enter our conscious mind. While we cannot explicitly observe the processing our subconscious performs, we can become more aware of the inputs and outputs. We can then use this awareness to influence and make interventions, for example in our reflex behaviours, information processing and emotional responses. In this way, over time, we can shape and harness more of the power of our subconscious.

Taking more control of your mind, both the conscious and subconscious, might seem challenging initially, but with practice it quickly gets easier and can become a permanent state that benefits from a virtuous cycle effect – that is, the more you take control, the more you want to, and are able to, take control.

OUR MINDS CRAVE 'COMFORT FOODS'

Our minds crave certain things, but too much of these things can be detrimental, in the same way physical cravings for fats and sugars can be detrimental to our health. For example, fats in small doses are essential and were crucial to the survival of our ancestors, as they allowed them to store energy between irregular meals. However, excess consumption of fats causes us to become weak and unhealthy. The key mind cravings to be aware of are:

- the need to be part of a team, group or tribe
- being uncomfortable with the unknown

- discomfort with conflicting ideas or knowledge
- a deep desire for and seeking of patterns
- taking mental shortcuts

Indulging excessively in these cravings can lead to our minds responding in a manner similar to our bodies' reaction to too much fat and sugar – they become unhealthy, leading to diminished life experiences. In the following sections we will explore the nature of these cravings and how to be more aware and minimise potential negative impacts, with specific exercises at the end of the chapter.

TEAM, GROUP, TRIBE

Our minds are compelled to want to be part of a team, group or tribe – but too much allegiance inevitability leads to an 'us' versus 'them' conflict. This could be between 'us' and 'other' groups or within our own group. Too much allegiance also results in a reduction of individual thoughts and suboptimal dogmatic groupthink-type decision-making.

There are clear benefits to this kind of team, group or tribe allegiance, not least in relation to the health of our minds. However, in general, the more our allegiance to the group increases, the more the benefits reduce and become increasingly outweighed by the downsides. We should be actively aware of the groups we are part of, and regularly monitor our relationship with those groups, to ensure we are effectively balancing the benefits and downsides and moderating our level of allegiance accordingly.

UNCOMFORTABLE WITH THE UNKNOWN

We are uncomfortable with the unknown, and we are compelled to seek answers to 'unknowns'. However, when the urge for answers or resolution of unknowns is too strong, it can cause us to lower our barriers of reasonable scepticism; in the worst-case scenario, we will believe anything and become entrenched in a confirmation bias spiral (see the section 'beyond our biases' in Chapter 5). For example, not knowing why there is a drought that has destroyed our harvest may cause us to become superstitious, attaching meaning to unrelated actions, ignoring contradictions and giving unwarranted weight to information that confirms our superstitions.

DISCOMFORT HOLDING CONFLICTING IDEAS IN OUR MINDS

We have a deep drive to minimise the discomfort of conflicting information, knowledge or ideas in our minds. This tendency is hard-wired and causes us to actively minimise any internal contradictions, either by bending the knowledge we have or by filtering new information through biases, to eliminate any potential contradictions to the existing knowledge in our minds. This tendency would have been vital for our ancestors to enable them to make rapid decisions with minimal cognitive effort. However, in our modern world this tendency is not always useful, and we can actually create significant mind strength when we embrace contradiction and complexity. Real understanding comes from understanding all information and perspectives.

It is often the case that the most powerful part of your knowledge is understanding what contradicts your interpretation or perspective and the nuance of those contradictions. Awareness of our tendency to shy away from shades of grey, and our blinkered striving for black and white, is crucial. Coupling this awareness with deliberately embracing the grey areas, and seeking to always understand what contradicts what we know, is vital to reduce the negative outcomes or impacts, no matter how uncomfortable that may feel.

We should also recognise the inertia to change our minds, both in ourselves and others, the discomfort and effort required is significant and disproportionate. However, when we actively recognise this, and do what is required to overcome this inertia, our ability to reach common ground and move forward collectively is significantly enhanced.

SEEKING PATTERNS

We seek and are stimulated by identifying patterns; however, our minds are so powerful and so predisposed to search for patterns that they may identify them where they do not, in fact, exist. For example, we can identify recognisable shapes or objects when looking at the clouds.

Our tendency to search for patterns is complemented by a phenomenon known as 'filling in', where our minds fill in missing information. For example, if you cover one eye, your mind will fill in the missing parts created by the blind spot. In fact, our brains are so powerful they can fill in details that we have never seen, such as leaves on a tree that is too far away to see. Generally, 'filling in' is processed in our subconscious without conscious knowledge or intent. It can happen rapidly, such as when survival depends on quick decisions, or retrospectively in the process of recalling memories.

Our tendency to seek and even desire patterns and our reliance on filling in can have potential downsides, since they are usually accompanied by a powerful sense of subjective certainty that we perceive as reality. This effect presents a risk of corrupting our interpretation of the information flowing into our minds and the resultant knowledge created or actions undertaken. We can see this manifest in conspiracy theories, where our deep desire to seek patterns, even when they do not exist, is a compelling and powerful force impacting our perceived reality. This effect is also compounded by our discomfort with the unknown, as discussed earlier in this section.

EXPECTATIONS

Like our tendency to seek and desire patterns, our expectations are powerful enough to influence our subjective perception and actual experience, such as with the 'placebo effect'. A fascinating example of the placebo effect is where a chemically inert substance can have an actual therapeutic effect only because we expect it to. This power of expectancy has been demonstrated using brain scanning technology, where our minds react to an expectation with the same neurochemical changes that would result if medication was actually administered. This effect is also experienced in reverse, known as the 'nocebo effect', where negative expectations lead to real negative outcomes. For example, the expectation of a medicine's side effects actually manifest even if the treatment is inert.

The placebo and nocebo effects are not isolated to medical treatments. Positive expectations of performance will increase confidence, which can then directly improve performance, for example in sports or public speaking. Another example could be the expectation of improving your productivity by upgrading to a new device; this expectation leads to increased focus and performance. Conversely, being told your environment is toxic could cause you to actually experience headaches, nausea or fatigue, even if the environment is not toxic at all.

THINKING SHORTCUTS: CO-OPTING KNOWLEDGE

The mind is immensely powerful and, in processing vast amounts of information in real time, has significant sophistication and energy needs. Since energy was a scarce resource for our ancestors, efficiency was crucial, and 'thinking shortcuts' were a good way to achieve this efficiency. Thinking shortcuts in our modern world are 'comfort foods' that masquerade as benign tricks to increase how quickly we can do things; however, their easy comforts can come with significant downsides. We started to explore these downsides in relation to information flow in Chapter 1, and we dig deeper into exploring biases, assumptions inferences and expectations in 'beyond our biases' Chapter 5.

A common thinking shortcut is our co-opting of knowledge or opinions without understanding or wanting to understand the foundation or framework on which they are based. Co-opting means treating someone else's knowledge or opinions as your own. This is common, may have no downside and in many contexts may be unavoidable – for example, knowing that the Himalayas are the tallest mountain range in the world.

However, when we co-opt knowledge, we are exposing ourselves to manipulation or negative outcomes, especially if we then use that knowledge to make choices, decisions or actions.

Therefore, when co-opting knowledge we should seek to be actively aware that our level of certainty of that knowledge is lower than if we had created it in our own minds; that is, combining objective information with our own experience and intuition.

Additionally, a keen awareness of when we are co-opting knowledge or opinions from a group, instead of from an individual, is particularly important. This is because in these situations we are more likely to suffer from groupthink and less likely to have a systematic foundation, and as such will have a lower knowledge certainty level. As we will explore in Chapter 3, knowledge certainty level is extremely important for understanding when we are making choices, decisions or actions based on this knowledge.

INDIVIDUAL VERSUS GROUP: THE CONTINUOUS STRUGGLE

Our conscious and subconscious minds are constantly trying to find the balance between the individual versus group impact of our choices, decisions and actions. While we are clearly individuals, we are also individuals who are part of a group. However, what benefits us as an individual may not benefit us as an individual who is part of a group. For example, the proceeds of a crime may benefit us individually, but at the same time, we want the crime to remain illegal because that benefits us as an individual who is a member of a society. Often, there is a trade-off that exists, even for the smallest decisions and actions.

We are constantly monitoring this individual–group dynamic, and continuously making interventions to iteratively change our approach and behaviours in real time. For example, there is the immediacy of joining a group that is responding to the destruction caused by a severe storm, or in the longer term leaving a group such as a cult because we think we are being diminished as an individual. It is important that we recognise this dynamic and that the two forces are in a symbiotic relationship. That is, we need both – us as individuals and us as part of a group – to thrive. We should actively maintain this awareness and make sure our perceptions and actions remain optimally calibrated – that is, that the balance between individual and group is right for us.

Consider, for example, someone supporting their sports team or being a member of cult. There is a trade-off between the individual benefits they receive and the downsides of spending all their time and money on these pursuits. Additionally, there is an opportunity cost, or the benefit they could be getting by doing something else. Compounding these issues, it becomes harder to objectively see trade-offs as an individual invests more time and resources in the group. This is known as a 'sunk cost fallacy' and can be expressed as 'throwing good money after bad', and is characterised by it becoming increasingly difficult to change course the more time and resources are 'sunk'.

KNOW WHAT YOU KNOW AND WHAT YOU DO NOT KNOW

The less you know, the less you know of what you do not know, and therefore, the more likely you are to think you know more than you do. This is known as the Dunning-Kruger effect[5] and is covered in the first section of Chapter 4.

To expand the concept, the less we know about something, the less we know about how little we know. This necessarily means we are likely to overestimate how much we know and underestimate how much we do not know. In general, the more information we receive and the more knowledge we build about a subject, the more awareness we have of how much we do not know.

While not immediately obvious, in reality all knowledge in our minds is in a 'beta' state – that is, in a constant state of potential iterative update. We should therefore be open to, and seek out, new information or changing contexts, as opposed to following our urges to 'lock down' our knowledge to avoid the discomfort of cognitive effort.

By challenging our knowledge and processing any contradictions that arise, even if that means accepting they may be unresolvable, we are actively increasing our certainty of knowledge and making our minds stronger.

When we strive to know all contradictions or refutable elements of our knowledge or opinions, we necessarily develop an in-depth awareness of all the weaknesses or shortcomings in our knowledge, or the information we base it on. Aspiring for and reaching this '360-degree' understanding of our knowledge and certainty levels is indicative of a deep mind strength.

Similar to a martial artist who has mastered a discipline, by understanding all sides of an argument, including knowledge, concepts, nuance or evidence, we are unlikely to engage in combat or trivial disagreements. The arduous work of building knowledge on all sides of an argument means you will inevitably waste less time in superfluous debate and instead spend your time on high-value activities, such as moving forward our collective understanding and knowledge.

STATE OF FLOW

We achieve a state of flow when we are focused on an activity and it feels almost effortless, such that we can lose track of time. The term 'flow' was first described by Mihaly Csikszentmihalyi in his 1990 book *Flow: The Psychology of Optimal Experience*.[6] In this context, flow can be thought of as effectively a resonance between our minds and an activity where we strike the right balance of feeling challenged but not overwhelmed and alignment with some sort of subjective purpose.

When in a state of flow, we feel a sense of comfort and reward from the activity we are performing, and it requires less energy to do that activity. In fact, in a state of flow we achieve a higher output. Seeking out and being aware of when we are in flow and how we get there is an important tool for our minds. Awareness of these conditions can help us orientate our minds and direct how we choose to spend our time.

INTELLIGENCES AND TRAITS

Our minds can be strong or weak regardless of our intelligence or personality traits; we can make them strong or let them be weak – it is a choice. Strong and weak minds exist across all intelligence domains and personality traits.

Understanding the intelligence domains and personality traits, together with a self-awareness of our own particular profile of intelligence and traits, is an extremely useful tool. It enables us to effectively and precisely strengthen our minds by informing where we want to focus our energy.

Intelligence exists across multiple domains in our minds. The traditional

'IQ' lens of intelligence, focused on logical-mathematical and linguistic intelligence, is a narrow perspective. We all have varying levels of intelligence across many domains, these can include but are not limited to the following:

- emotional intelligence: a conjunction of interpersonal and intrapersonal intelligence that implies the ability to recognise and manage our own and other people's emotions
- kinaesthetic or bodily intelligence: the ability to use the whole body or parts of the body to solve problems through a deep mind–body bond, achieve great control of automatic and voluntary movements or use the body in a highly differentiated and competent way, such as in the case of athletes, dancers, surgeons, mechanics, physical therapists and carpenters
- linguistic intelligence: a deep resonance with spoken and written language, generally manifesting as a fluency in learning languages and an ability to use language to optimally achieve your intended outcomes
- logical mathematical intelligence: the ability to analyse problems rationally, perform mathematical operations and investigate scientific questions
- musical intelligence: the sensitivity, interpretation and composition of musical patterns, and the ability to recognise and create musical tones, rhythms and timbres
- interpersonal intelligence: understanding others' intentions, desires and deeper motivations, often accompanied by the ability to leverage those understandings for more effective outcomes, whether positive or nefarious
- intrapersonal intelligence: this is fundamentally inward, since it implies the ability to understand ourselves, being aware of our ambitions, feelings and moods and using that information to intelligently manage our lives
- naturalistic intelligence: a rich perception of the relationships between

species, recognising possible differences or similarities generally with people as the primary comparative subject

- spatial intelligence: a rich awareness and dexterity with patterns across our perceived space, including wide expanses such as those used by navigators, as well as on a more human scale as embodied by architects, surgeons or sculptors
- digital technological intelligence: the proficiency in understanding, using, and interacting with digital technologies and computer systems.
- existential intelligence: the ability to locate ourselves with respect to the cosmos, recognise existential features of our outlook and reflect on existence and the meaning of life
- creative intelligence: using imagination to create original ideas, as espoused by musicians, designers or artists, often resulting in new or highly innovative concepts, work or products
- collaborative intelligence: being able to work with others and share knowledge and ways of doing things to achieve a common goal

Engaging in self-reflection and analysis to try to determine our own individual intelligence levels in each domain of intelligence can be extremely useful. This self-awareness informs us of our relative strengths, which in turn helps us shape how and where we want to focus our time and energy, especially in relation to strengthening our minds.

Intelligence type is a crucial lens to help us understand how our minds work, but an equally important lens is personality traits. Considering both lenses is critical both to exploring ourselves and understanding others, putting ourselves in their shoes to understand their perspective. While they are completely distinct lenses, they are, of course, highly inter-related and have a complex relationship that is likely unique to each of our minds. Each of our minds has a distinct set of personality traits, and this variation and uniqueness is a huge benefit to us all since it means there is huge diversity across minds. For example, this diversity will drive completely different approaches to activities like problem-solving.

A good starting point to understanding our common personality traits is known as the 'Big 5' – the table below shows the Big 5 and some of their characteristics.

'Big 5' Trait	Trait Spectrum	High Score	Low Score
Conscientiousness	Disorganised vs Disciplined	Careful	Impulsive
Agreeableness	Uncooperative vs Trusting	Helpful	Suspicious
Neuroticism	Confident vs Anxious	Pessimistic	Calm
Openness to Experiences	Practical Vs Imaginative	Spontaneous	Prefers Routine
Extroversion	Thoughtful vs Sociable	Fun-loving	Reserved

In each of our minds, we have elements of all these traits to different degrees. The Big 5 are thought to capture the broad dimensions of human personality variation. Understanding whether each trait is more or less dominant in our own mind is an important foundation. Self-awareness of our trait profile will inform, for example, how and why we enjoy or do not enjoy certain things and why and inform where we may choose to focus our mind-strengthening efforts.

While these definitions are a useful guide, they are also an oversimplification. Our own individual combination of traits and intelligence types is significantly more complex than these high-level 'bucket' definitions. The sophistication of these definitions and our collective understanding and self-awareness will no doubt continue to develop in years to come. These definitions are also particularly at risk of being misunderstood or miscommunicated because our related experiences only exist in our own consciousness and, therefore, only we can describe them. We explore some of the challenges around our ability to effectively communicate the subjective experience of our conscious minds further in Chapter 5. It is also useful to consider how a combination of genetic, environmental and cultural factors can play a role in shaping our minds; for example, culture may have either an encouraging or a repressing impact on how certain traits are expressed.

CRITICAL THINKING

Critical thinking refers to our ability to analyse information objectively and make a reasoned judgement. Generally, this requires the evaluation of evidence such as data, facts, observations or studies. Critical thinking is inherent in our minds and is used every day to help us decide what, how and why we are going to do what we do. However, with practice and training, critical thinking can be significantly enhanced. The stronger our ability to think critically, the lower the likelihood of errors as we process information, create knowledge and make decisions or take actions that have consequences.

Considering the veracity or reliability of information or evidence is a crucial element of critical thinking, including what it is and where it comes from, such as determining the objectivity of a source. You are more effective in your critical thinking when you consider multiple sources, whether the information or evidence is consistent with your experience, and are aware of your potential biases, as explored in Chapter 5.

When evaluating theories or concepts, understanding the attempts that have been made to disprove them is crucial; in fact, determining if it is even possible to disprove them is a mandatory first consideration. If it is impossible to disprove something, there is immediately an upper ceiling to the level of certainty that can ever be obtained. We explore certainty levels in more detail in Chapter 3. Another key element to evaluating theories or concepts is understanding how compatible those theories are with existing proven theories or concepts; these can usually provide a useful structure that helps with corroborating or disproving them.

A simple framework for critical thinking is proposed in the exercise section of this chapter, constituting observation, analysis, inference and generating conclusions. This is one approach to help guide the analysis of quantitative or qualitative information or evidence to determine veracity and reliability, and can be helpful to corroborate or disprove theories or concepts. Whichever approach you use, critical thinking is a fundamental capability, the importance of which cannot be overstated. We should all be continually seeking to improve our critical thinking skills and helping others to develop and master these capabilities.

INHERENT SUBJECTIVITY OF OUR MINDS

Recognising our subjectivity and understanding that everyone has their own subjective perspective is an important core mind strength, especially understanding how subjectivity can impact the flow of information and the transfer of the quality of knowledge.

A good example demonstrating the power of our inherent subjectivity, is the experience of being thrown forward in a car when you slam on the brakes. While it absolutely feels like you have been flung forward and that you need the seatbelt to secure you, this is not what has happened. In reality, the speed at which your body is traveling has not changed and you have not been flung forward, but rather the car has changed speed, and the seatbelt is pulling you back to the new speed of the car. This is a useful metaphor to apply to all our experiences and perceptions because it illustrates the power of our subjectivity, and why we should therefore always be alert to how it acts as a filter for the information flowing into our minds and how we process it.

The inherent subjectivity of our minds has a pervasive impact on both the information we provide to others and the information that flows into our minds. We cannot eliminate these effects, but if we are actively aware of them and sensitive to how they manifest, we can manage and mitigate the impact these effects have on our choices, decisions and actions.

When we seek to identify the essence of an issue, we should focus exclusively on what is in front of us. This includes actively ignoring our expectations, since they will likely inhibit our effective discovery of the essence of an idea, argument or piece of information. If we find it difficult to completely ignore our expectations, which is very common, challenging and understanding our expectations is often a more effective technique. By doing this, we will at least be aware of the impact of our expectations; we explore this further in the Chapter 5 section on 'Beyond Our Biases'.

PERSPECTIVE

Our minds' ability to change perspective is extremely important. Changing perspective from one of pure subjectivity to increasing levels of objectivity and even putting ourselves in the shoes of others is extremely powerful.

Developing the ability to always look at information from multiple points of view means we will develop more neural pathways. This increased neural activity significantly increases the likelihood of generating better ideas and getting better outcomes. In the worst case, exploring different perspectives will only reinforce and give more support to a purely subjective perspective. However, it is more likely that this exploration will generate increasingly resilient, innovative and sophisticated outcomes.

Chapter 6 explores how we can use perspectives in more detail. We will focus here on 'zoom in and out', which is a specific type of changing perspective. It is particularly powerful for managing stress and increasing productivity. Zooming out describes the act of stepping outside of your immediate micro-focus to understand the bigger picture. A good analogy may be a conductor of an orchestra, who zooms in on a violin melody but then zooms out to hear and comprehend the orchestra's symphony as a whole, or the 'pinch to zoom' functionality commonly used on touch screen devices today, originally developed at the University of Delaware in the late 1980s. Zooming out helps take you out of your current mindset, diminishing what may appear insurmountable and aiding your understanding of the transient nature of things. Highly creative and productive people tend to be characterised by an ability to zoom in and out quickly on a frequent basis. This is because they can create solutions that address both micro and macro challenges simultaneously.

IDEAS

Ideas can exist independently of one person or one mind; they can exist objectively, encoded or written down. However, since we each have our own subjective interpretation of an idea, and some ideas are very compelling, we can become too attached and lose the ability to continue to challenge and interrogate ideas objectively. This means suboptimal ideas can continue to be given too much prominence in our minds, which can lead to suboptimal actions and outcomes. Worse than this, we can perceive the challenge of ideas by others as challenges or attacks on us personally, which diminishes the likelihood of constructive discourse and the development, refinement or improvement of ideas. We explore ways of improving how we think and challenge the ideas of others, and the ideas in our minds, in the exercises section at the end of this chapter.

INTUITION

Intuition is a powerful force within our minds that guides us towards understanding or making decisions, seemingly without the use of conscious reasoning or logic. While we do not know exactly how it works, it is understood that the subconscious mind is responsible and draws on our past experiences, knowledge and emotions to provide us with a 'gut feeling' or insight that is often difficult to articulate. This process is a result of our subconscious minds constantly processing enormous amounts of information; however, we can become more aware of when we are using or ignoring our subconscious by training our conscious minds.

Intuition is a critical core component of a strong mind: the more we are actively aware and able to nurture and cultivate our intuition, the more effective we will be at building knowledge and the resulting navigation of our lives in a rewarding manner.

Intuition is extremely helpful for enabling us to make quick and accurate judgements and generate insights and hunches. This is particularly helpful in making sense of complex contexts and situations. Awareness of these gut feelings and insights, and the signals our physical body sends us, allows us to tap into the wisdom provided by our intuition. It also helps us monitor where it may not be entirely useful to us in our modern context, so we can ultimately make better choices, decisions and actions.

EXERCISES

Some of these exercises are challenging at first, but as you think deeply and even wrestle with the concepts, you will notice marked improvements and will be able to return to them again and again, each time strengthening your neural pathways. Experiment with different ways of exercising and see which techniques work best for you:

- Explore in your mind – try it with your eyes closed or while doing physical exercise.
- Write down your thoughts, draw concepts or talk out loud to yourself.
- Work with others in dialogue.

You Have Full Control

- Tell yourself: 'I am in complete control of my mind':
  1. If it doesn't feel like it, or if this has made no difference, say it again, but really try to seize control and truly believe what you are saying.
  2. Say it again, until you are convinced by what you are saying. Ask yourself out loud, 'Do you get it?' and embrace the dawning realisation that you, and only you, are in control!
  3. Deliberately try and capture this feeling and remember what this sense of empowerment feels like. Do this exercise regularly.
- Over time, it will go from a short-term realisation to a more sustained sense of self and, ultimately, will become your day-to-day mindset.

Team, Group, Tribe

- Reflect on your membership of any teams, groups or tribes and consider whether they are active or passive memberships. Ask yourself the following questions:
  1. What do they want or need me to think?
  2. What do they need or get from me?

3. How much and what do I give to the group?

4. To what extent am I diminished as an individual when I am in this group?

5. Does the group claim authority above that of my individual autonomy?

6. Is the challenge 'on what authority' used to assert that the individual's authority is less than the group's authority?

- These questions should help you assess the balance of benefits versus downsides and where you may want to moderate over-consumption of this mind craving.

Uncomfortable With the Unknown

- Imagine you just became aware of a new fundamental 'unknown' in your life:

  1. What would you seek to do to try and understand it?

  2. To what extent would you seek evidence that helped explain it, and how much would you want to believe that evidence?

- Can you think of examples of others being uncomfortable with 'unknowns' and as a result avoiding them or being content with a much lower quality of information, thus reducing the level of challenge that they would usually have and minimising any reasonable scepticism?

  1. Does this include others lowering their scepticism and embracing weak evidence but managing to convince themselves they have a high knowledge certainty level?

  2. Does confirmation bias (see Chapter 5) lead them to filter out contradictory information and only embrace information that supports their existing knowledge or opinion?

  3. What do you think they could do to be more comfortable with the reality of the unknown? What would these techniques look like in practice?

  4. Where the discomfort of the unknown causes others to lower their

standards, does this leave them vulnerable to manipulation or exploitation by others, whether that is inadvertently or nefarious?

5. Consider whether any of your thoughts on others' uncomfortableness with the unknown could also apply to you.

- Now challenge yourself – are there things that you are uncomfortable with not knowing?

1. What do you do with this discomfort?

2. Do you ever have a high degree of certainty but the evidence is sparse?

3. How do you seek to minimise your discomfort? How much are you likely to lower your barriers of scepticism in order to provide an explanation for an 'unknown'?

4. What techniques could you use to ensure that your discomfort does not drive you to compromise on your standards?

Discomfort Holding Conflicting Ideas in Our Minds

- Undertake a thought experiment. Try to hold two competing ideas in your mind at the same time. For example, something trivial could be: you love going shopping on the high street but you actually buy things online. Or much more seriously: you do not want people to starve but you know there are starving people. Try using some of your own examples while working though these exercises:

1. How does it feel to interrogate both ideas concurrently?

2. How do you deal with the urge to try to reconcile the two ideas rather than explore the discomfort of accepting both as truths?

3. Is this an experience you recognise as happening regularly?

4. How often do you think there are examples of things that conflict with the ideas, values or knowledge in your mind?

5. How much do you think you embrace steps to minimise discomfort by bending or distorting information to support an explanation to convince yourself and others?

6. Practise holding contradictions in your mind; over time, the discomfort will lessen as your mind gets stronger. Similar to the first time you undertake physical exercise, it is uncomfortable, but with practice, it turns into a comfortable and even fulfilling activity.

7. Try to regularly and deliberately seek out, as a matter of course, anything that contradicts or conflicts with the ideas, values or knowledge in your mind, so you can fully embrace and understand it.

8. When was the last time you changed your mind?

9. When you change your mind about something, actively recognise the inherent inertia and discomfort in doing this, what does it feel like - how do you mitigate and overcome the discomfort?

10. Practice changing your mind regularly, and think about how you can apply these observations more broadly to your day to day, and also how you can help others (friend or foe) when you see them going through similar discomfort?

Seeking Patterns

- Consider patterns that you experience as subjective reality but do not exist:
  1. identifying faces in food like toast, sliced vegetables or fruits (known as pareidolia)
  2. experiencing pareidolia by seeing faces in plug sockets, on staplers or even in wood grain
  3. seeing recognisable shapes or objects in spilled liquids or food stains on clothing
- How powerful is your perception of this effect? While these examples are trivial, if the context was more serious, what steps could you take to minimise the impact on your subjective reality?
- Think about how this seeking of patterns can affect our perception of

the information flow, particularly where there are unknowns or a lack of information or evidence:

1. How strong do you think the tendency is to identify patterns or connections, even where there are none?

2. Try creating your own patterns or connections that are not real and test them with others. Are you surprised that they can be considered even slightly plausible?

3. Consider some examples of conspiracy theories that vary in terms of their plausibility. How much do you think they can be explained by our deep desire to identify patterns and connections?

4. How can you ensure you are actively aware of when you are identifying patterns and connections which do not exist?

5. Can you develop strategies that work for you to intervene, or tools to test if the pattern or connection is actually real – refer to the critical thinking exercises in this chapter.

- Consider that while we know that the power of seeking patterns can alter our subjective reality, this may make us more susceptible to conspiracy theories, which are characterised by providing seemingly clear explanations for complex or unclear events.

- Consider if the below activities, which are associated with conspiracy theories, are a result of our innate desire to seek patterns:

1. connecting disparate pieces of information together in a complex narrative that creates a 'hidden truth'

2. weaving together various pieces of data or events to construct a coherent but essentially unsupported explanation

3. selecting supporting information or evidence while dismissing or ignoring anything contradictory

4. encouragement and validation by like-minded individuals connecting and reinforcing each other's beliefs in communities and echo chambers

5. doubling down on the conspiracy theory, resulting in even more

elaborate reasoning and construction of explanations, triggered by information or evidence that contradicts the conspiracy theory – consider the previous section on discomfort with holding conflicting ideas.

Expectations

* Think about how much the placebo or nocebo effects can be potentially helpful or a hindrance for you.
* Are you aware of any examples in your own experience of either placebo or nocebo effects? Were you aware that your perception of reality had been altered at the time? If not, when did you realise?
* Consider some examples you have noticed in others where you have seen a placebo or nocebo effect:
  1. How different was their subjective perception or physical experience from objective reality?
  2. At what point did they become aware, if ever, and what caused this awareness to take hold?
  3. To what extent did the awareness diminish the impact of the placebo or nocebo effect?
  4. Where the placebo was causing positive outcomes, could it be maintained even when there was awareness it was a placebo?
* Consider some relatively benign placebo-like effects:
  1. For example, even if you do not have one, pretending to start the day with a positive mindset, and expressing that you are feeling good, can often influence those you interact with and lead to a virtuous cycle where the outcomes are actually better than without the positive mindset, and vice versa with a negative outlook.
  2. Similarly, consider examples such as lucky charms or sporting rituals that cause a positive expectation that can often be self-perpetuating.

- Apply the placebo and nocebo effects to your information flow. To what extent do you think the content and tone of the information flow can impact your perception and influence your subjective view of reality?

  1. Consider an overly negative information flow, such as doom scrolling – could this lead you to make decisions that are then self-perpetuating? For example, could it lead to you not getting out of bed because you are scared and overwhelmed, not striving for what you want and treating others badly, who then treat you badly?

- Consider what you think about deliberately using placebo effects to provide positive outcomes and what that may mean for inadvertently creating conditions for nocebo effects.

Shortcuts: Co-opting Knowledge

- Consider how knowledge is created in our minds, exploring the key concepts and potential pitfalls set out in Chapter 3

- Interrogate yourself honestly – try to identify knowledge that you consider to have been created in your own mind (i.e. by combining information, experience and intuition), but in fact has actually been formed outside of your mind:

  1. You should expect a significant number of examples, because in our modern world we have easy access to incredible amounts of information, much of which is impossible to combine with our experience or intuition.

  2. Consider the range of your knowledge that been co-opted. How do you use this knowledge to drive your choices, decisions or actions? Focus on this knowledge and consider:

     - Does this knowledge need to be co-opted? What are the limiting factors – for example, no experience, lack of information or an intuition blind spot?

- What can you do to increase the certainty of your knowledge and reduce the extent to which it is co-opted?

- Reflect on the choices, decisions or actions you make based on this knowledge. Are they all in your interest, or do they benefit others who are the source of the co-opted knowledge? Is there encouragement, actively or passively, to not challenge the co-opted knowledge?

Individual Versus Group: The Continuous Struggle

- Consider the key dynamic – both the individual and the group are in a symbiotic relationship. That is, they rely on each other.

- Think about when the relationship is skewed towards either party, imagining it as a tug of war. What is the cost if there is an imbalance, for both the individual and the group?

- Try to determine the contexts, in your life and for others, where the group–individual dynamic is most important. This will likely be when it drives choices, actions or decisions:

  1. For these situations, consider ways you can be more actively aware of the dynamic.

  2. Think about steps you can take to address situations where the dynamic is not balanced. For example, if there is a high imbalance in favour of the group, this may involve an individual leaving the group if that individual is being diminished or even exploited. Or if the imbalance is less significant in either the group or individual's favour, the solution may involve simple actions such as giving more time, energy and resources to the group or to the individual.

Know What You Know and What You Do Not Know

- Try to instil a recuring behaviour to constantly challenge yourself, colloquially known as playing 'devil's advocate'. Aim to trigger the challenge to yourself when you are using knowledge to make a choice, decision or action by creating a sense of excitement in the discovery.

- Leverage this healthy scepticism of your own knowledge to help with validating where you have high certainty levels and where you do not. Are you comfortable with low certainty levels and, if not, what will do you to increase them?

- Practise the habit of seeking knowledge that contradicts your assumed wisdom and aspire for a '360-degree' understanding of your knowledge. Important considerations include:

  1. If you are utterly convinced of your knowledge, it is a good indication that you have not considered everything.

  2. Just because you think you are absolutely correct, and are utterly convinced you are absolutely correct, does not mean you are correct.

  3. Our convictions, no matter how intoxicating, are not correlated to veracity or accuracy. It is entirely possible to be unexcited and unconvinced over knowledge where we actually have a high certainty level, and vice versa – utterly convinced about knowledge where our certainty levels are low. This is why it is so important to be consciously aware of our knowledge certainty levels, as we will explore in Chapter 3.

  4. Absolute certainty, without nuance or clarity of possible contradictions, is usually an indication that we have not considered relevant information or have subjectively filtered information; this is explored further in Chapter 5.

- Try to avoid the temptation to force an answer where there is not one. We have a tendency to do this, often driven by our discomfort with the unknown and holding conflicting ideas in our minds.

- Knowing what you do not know (the 'unknowns') is as important as knowing what you do know, and is critical for core mind strength:

  1. Identify some examples of 'unknowns' that resonate with you,

including things that are both significant and trivial, and those that you are familiar with and also those where you have little frame of reference. For example, the James Webb telescope is now revealing giant supernovae that defy some of our known science.

2. Explore your examples. Are you content with not knowing the answers? If not, why not?

3. Consider the tendency for you or others to require less evidence than usual when faced with an 'unknown'. Does the comfort of answering an unknown, through weak certainty levels or weak evidence, actually help us? Is ignorance really bliss or a trap?

State of Flow

- Deliberately reflect on and familiarise yourself with examples of times you have had the subjective qualitative experience of being in flow – that is, focused on an activity in such a way it feels almost effortless and you lose track of time.

- Try to develop your self-awareness of when you are in flow:
    1. Keep an active awareness and write down the contexts and factors that are present when you are in flow, even if this is in hindsight.
    2. Once you've identified a fairly good picture of the factors and context that contribute to your flow, test it out and refine it until you have a clear understanding of what flow means to you.
    3. Embrace those conditions and share them with others – do they agree, based on what they know about you?
    4. Consider also what seems to be your counter-flow, which is the opposite experience to flow; this can be helpful with validating the factors and context that are optimal for you to be in flow.

- As you capture examples of your counter-flow, where the activity is arduous and time seems to crawl, rank these and determine strategies to mitigate or avoid the most severe of these examples.

- Use your understanding of your flow and counter-flow to make choices and cultivate contexts that allow you to resonate at the highest frequency. For example, are your passions, relationships, job, ways of doing things, health and diet and hobbies, and the groups surrounding you, optimal for you?

- Help others identify and maximise their flow. This will likely make you feel good but also make you better at optimising your own flow, in line with the methodology previously discussed of 'see one, do one, teach one'.

Intelligences and Traits

- Reflect on your own intelligences and traits and ask others to corroborate and take assessments to support an objective identification.

- Once you have a clearer picture of your intelligences and traits, including where you may be stronger or weaker, explore how you could make life choices that are informed by this knowledge. For example:

  1. Where will you get the most bang for your buck? Can you nudge yourself into environments and situations that play to your strengths or away from your weaknesses?

  2. Where there are weaknesses, be proactive and honest with others about them. You might not get stronger, but reducing the risk of others misinterpreting you is certainly of value.

  3. Find out about the intelligences and traits of other important people in your life; this will help improve communication and allow you to help each other, and avoid wasting time doing things or communicating at cross purposes.

Critical Thinking

Explore the simple critical thinking framework below and consider if it makes sense to you as a theory – do you broadly recognise these four stages from your day-to-day activities? If not, think about what may be inhibiting you.

- Observation involves the collection of information and evidence, mainly through noticing and absorbing information, and is the foundation of critical thinking.
- The second stage is analysis of information and evaluation of evidence or data. It is important to consider all the following steps, but direct your attention as relevant to the topic, idea or knowledge:

1. Evaluation of quantitative data. This is data that can be counted or measured, like drums in a drum kit or votes in an election:
   - Consider numerical statistical analysis, such as determining the range, frequency and minimum and maximum values within a dataset and measures of average like the mean, mode and median.
   - Quantitative data can be used to provide very strong support to corroborate or disprove a hypothesis.

2. Evaluation of qualitative data:
   - Qualitative data is dynamic and subjective in nature and usually descriptive – for example, feelings or opinions. It is usually unstructured and can take the form of words, such as surveys or interviews.
   - It is important to consider that qualitative data is usually open to interpretation, and compared to quantitative data is particularly helpful for answering 'why' and 'how' questions.
   - However, qualitative data is, in general, weaker compared with quantitative data in terms of its ability to corroborate or disprove a hypothesis. We explore this further in the 'qualitative data' section in Chapter 4.

3. Unpicking and analysis of any reasoning or logic in the topic, idea or knowledge: be aware that faulty reasoning or logic can undermine and distort even the most supported, accurate and comprehensive data or information.

4. Ensure you do not rush to judgement and be aware our minds

tend to want to do this.

5. Jumping to conclusions is highly likely to lead to simplistic and inaccurate outcomes, usually containing errors based on assumptions about:
    - other people's thoughts and feelings
    - group stereotypes
    - speculation about future events.

- Drawing inferences involves forming an opinion or drawing conclusions based on the information, evidence and outcomes of your analysis and evaluation. Important considerations include:
    1. our tendency to assume correlation is representative of causation, and any errors flowing from this potentially erroneous assumption
    2. ensuring we consider any potential impact from bias, assumptions and expectation; we explore how to identify and manage these potential traps in Chapter 5.

- Combining your observations, analyses, evaluations and inferences to create potential conclusions or determine what further information, evidence, clarifications, corroborations or mutivariate analyses may be required.

Inherent Subjectivity of Our Minds

- Reflect on the example of being thrown forward in a car when you slam the brakes on:
    1. How real does this feel, and what does it feel like to understand that your perception of reality was false?
    2. Familiarise yourself with this feeling and the experience of understanding the power of your subjectivity, and think of other examples that you can relate to.
    3. As you explore these examples and the dynamic between subjective and objective experiences, you should find it increasingly familiar; this is your mind becoming stronger. In

time, it will become almost straightforward to 'flip' back and forth between subjective and objective perspectives.

4. Try to use this 'flip' technique to monitor and filter your information flow, asking yourself questions about your filtering. This helps challenge the effects of the inherent subjectivity of your mind. Questions could include 'How much is my subjective interpretation or filtering actually changing the essence of the information?' and 'Do I have a relationship with the knowledge that is skewing my ability look at it objectively?'

- Practise being more self-aware of your subjectivity, whether in interactions with others or using examples from your information flow. Try using an example to be actively aware of your expectations, then manage those expectations, and then try ignoring them.

- Consider how our expectations can get in the way of discovering the essence of a topic or idea, because they limit our objective thinking. In particular, consider how much we are impacted by what others have told us about how we should be observing, interpreting or evaluating information.

- Given we cannot eliminate the effects of inherent subjectivity, think about the following:

1. Can you be more actively aware and sensitive to how these effects manifest?

2. What would you want to do to manage and mitigate the impact inherent subjectivity has on your choices, decisions and actions?

3. Are you able to actually manage and mitigate in these ways? If so, are they techniques you want to make habitual and, if so, how can you seek to successfully embed them in your normal behaviours?

Perspective

- Experiment with flipping a situation from your perspective to someone else's and then out to a completely objective third person:

1. Try this on a few examples, real or hypothetical. Does this provide you with any insight or ideas not previously obvious to you?

2. How difficult is it to do this and what are the challenges?

3. Work through these challenges systematically. Are there techniques you can use to overcome them? For example, employing more or less empathy, doing research to bolster your understanding of other contexts or engaging in real dialogue to understand how someone else is subjectively experiencing things through their perspective.

4. Try to develop a shorthand way of doing this 'flipping' in your mind so it becomes more automatic. As you practise, you will likely become quicker and more effective as you develop more neural pathways and are able to quickly draw on your expertise in considering things from multiple points of view.

- Practise 'zooming in and out':

1. Imagine stepping outside of your immediate micro-focus to see the bigger picture.

2. Good analogies are seeing the wood for the trees or, more literally, zooming out of a map or out of our solar system, and then back in. Also try to visualise the concept through the 'pinch-to-zoom' gesture commonly used on touchscreens today.

3. Try using your mind's ability to zoom out as a tool to contextualise events taking place by zooming out and seeing them in a broader context, such as the whole project, your whole career, your whole life or even the whole universe.

4. While zooming in and out, it is important not to diminish your experience, the events that are happening or how you feel. However, while fully embracing the reality of these experiences, at the same time zoom out to see the experiences in a much wider context.

5. This wider context achieved through zooming allows the events

to be understood as transitory, and even compartmentalised. This can help increase resilience by allowing you to understand a more objective perspective via realisations such as 'things will pass' or the idea of letting the situation flow through and ultimately past you.

6. Now consider zooming in and out as a tool to enable you to increase your productivity:

   • Fully 'zoomed out', you can consider all the things you want or need to do and consider them strategically based on priority and resources needed.

   • Then 'zoom in' to focus on a specific activity so you can dedicate your full cognitive resources to it, instead of being overwhelmed by everything you want and need to do, all at the same time.

   • Practising this until it becomes second nature, such that you can zoom in and out quickly, regularly and when you want to, will enable you to address both micro and macro challenges and solutions simultaneously. For example, imagine a car production line, zooming in to a specific part of the assembly and then zooming out to the whole line. Now apply the analogy to your life, project or task.

Ideas

• Think of some examples of ideas that you are attached to. Consider a range across trivial, profound, emotional and practical genres. Taking each word at a time, consider the following:

1. Experiment with considering the idea as a floating thing outside of you. Visualise it such that you can imagine prodding it.

2. Can you disassociate yourself from the idea and remove emotional attachments, such that you are able to truly objectively appreciate the idea's strengths and weaknesses and identify where

improvement or development may be possible?

3. Ask yourself if you can be more objective about how you think about the idea – at what point does your subjectivity creep in?

4. Is the subjectivity valid or irrelevant? If it is irrelevant, what happens if you move to a more objective perspective?

5. Consider when others challenge your ideas – do you perceive it as a constructive way to collectively move the idea forward and develop it, either in substance or sophistication, or do you see it as a personal challenge or attack on your idea?

6. Do you agree with the assertion that suboptimal ideas can be given too much prominence in our minds, which can lead to suboptimal actions and outcomes?

7. If you do, consider what you think you need to do to challenge and interrogate your ideas objectively, particularly where they are driving your actions.

8. Try to explain the concept of disassociating yourself from an idea to someone else; this can be a good way to increase your own ability.

9. Consider the challenges of removing emotional attachments to an idea, and also the hazard of considering an idea to be flawless – would this decrease the likelihood of you wanting to challenge it?

Intuition

•   Think about your own intuition:

1. Are you aware of when you are using it and, in particular, of when it is disproportionately driving your actions?

2. Do you value the wisdom provided, and do you see any dangers in relying on it too much?

3. Consider what you can do to become more aware. Write down important decisions or actions you have taken in the last month, then, with the benefit of hindsight, think about how much

involvement intuition had with the outcome.

4. Think about examples you see in others where their decisions, choices or actions seem to be overwhelmingly driven by intuition. Are there parallels with actions you have taken? Consider what you can to do ensure you are aware if this is happening.

Chapter 3.
Building Your Foundation

Knowledge = Information + Experience + Intuition

Individually, each of us holds and creates knowledge within our minds. We exhibit strong confidence in some aspects of this knowledge while being less certain about others. Determining our level of certainty regarding the knowledge we possess is crucial, as it shapes our decision-making and actions.

FIGURE 4

The level of certainty of knowledge in our minds can be thought of as a sliding scale, from 0% to 99% (see Figure 4). In fact, the upper limit is the highest number you can think of that is less than 100%. Recognising that it is impossible to ever be 100% certain about any knowledge is fundamentally important, and we explore this further below. It is also hugely empowering – *you* are in control of working out the relative certainty of whatever knowledge *you* have. Three critical elements underpin this foundation:

1. Absolute certainty: it is impossible to be 100% certain of any knowledge.
2. Spectrum of certainty: there is a level of certainty for each element of our knowledge.
3. The fallacy of a lack of certainty: it is wrong to equate a lack of absolute certainty with the idea that everything is equally unknown.

ABSOLUTE CERTAINTY

Our thoughts only exist in our minds, and therefore, there is always a possibility, no matter how small, that what we think we know is not true or even real. For example, while highly unlikely, there is a possibility we could be in a dream or in a simulation, or even something as far-fetched as being controlled by aliens! Inherently, because our consciousness only exists in our own minds, we can never be 100% certain of any knowledge or experience.

For instance, if someone told you it was 2 p.m., there are several ways to verify this information. You could look at the daylight outside, consider if you have recently eaten lunch, consult a watch, and so on. While all these sources of information and considerations will get you extremely close to knowing if it is 2 p.m., they can never give you 100% certainty. This is because you can only create this knowledge and experience it in your consciousness. Your consciousness only exists in your mind, and therefore, inherently, the potential always exists that it is not 100% objectively true or even real.

THE SPECTRUM OF CERTAINTY

We have full autonomy to exercise our minds and increase the level of certainty of our knowledge. By actively taking control of our minds, we can seek to understand the certainty of the range of knowledge we hold in our minds. We can make a deliberate effort, when we want to, to try to increase the level of certainty of specific areas of our knowledge. We explore this throughout this book, in particular in the chapters on Tuning Your Mind's Ear (Chapter 4) and Core Mind Strength (Chapter 2) and the accompanying exercises.

It is important for our minds to work out and understand where our knowledge certainty sits on the sliding scale of 0–99%. This is especially true where that knowledge is driving choices, decisions or actions that have consequences. Key considerations in working out our knowledge certainty include:

- Understanding the quality and context of the information flowing into our minds by asking ourselves, is there any:
    1. corruption or noise in the information flow (refer to Chapter 4: Tuning Your Mind's Ear)
    2. unintentional or deliberate interference, for example caused by nefarious actors
    3. susceptibility of the information to bias, assumptions, inference errors and expectation distortions.
- Being aware of how our experience and intuition combine with information to create our knowledge. For example, if we have no experience in the area and are therefore only relying on information and intuition, this will usually result in knowledge that has a lower certainty level.

We can increase our mind strength by developing clarity about what we know and the certainty level of that knowledge, and, crucially, knowing what we do not know. This self-awareness is critical to ensure we are fully aware when we have a low level of knowledge certainty, since in these circumstances we are more vulnerable to making errors in choices, decisions or actions and at higher risk of potential manipulation by others. Conversely, the more we seek to increase the certainty level of our knowledge, the higher our certainty levels are likely to become, and the more likely we are to make better choices, decisions and actions.

A common reason for us having a low level of knowledge certainty is that the knowledge or opinions have not been formed in our own minds. We will of course routinely receive knowledge or opinions like this, but we need to be actively aware that they will always be of a low level of knowledge certainty; this is particularly important if we use that information to make choices, decisions or actions that have consequences.

However, by using our own minds to consider the information, evidence and rationale, or understand the critical thinking that the knowledge or opinions are based on, we can usually increase our knowledge certainty level. If we do not seek to do this, and we have knowledge or opinions that have not been formed in our own minds and that we then use to make choices, decisions or actions, there is a higher risk of manipulation by others and errors in our judgements and actions.

Ultimately, if we are going to make choices, decisions or actions based on our knowledge, 80% certainty is vastly different from 1%. We should therefore work out what is the actual knowledge in our minds and what is our level of certainty of that knowledge.

Use *your mind* to work it out so *you know* what you know. Deliberate effort is required to understand and increase our knowledge certainty levels.

However, as with training for your body, when you exercise your mind, it gets stronger. Never stop reminding yourself that *you* are the only one who has control of your mind, and *you* have complete freedom to work out:

- how you want to think about things
- how you digest information
- how information and evidence affect your knowledge
- how your knowledge affects whether you act and what action you take

Understanding that the conclusions and opinions in our minds are temporary and constantly changing is crucial for utilising them in decision-making and actions. Our minds have the capacity to generate new conclusions and opinions as circumstances change, leading to ongoing contradictions.

Recognising and embracing these contradictions can radically increase our awareness of our certainty of knowledge, including whether it is high or low or moving higher or lower. When we harness this awareness and use it to base our conclusions or opinions in the context of all the competing variables or knowledge, we significantly increase the likelihood of better decisions, choices and actions.

We have a tendency to become wedded to opinions, since it is generally easier to regurgitate rather than reconsider inputs, context or rationale. In many ways, in the context of a video of the totality of your life, an opinion is comparable to only a photo. A photo captures a moment, defined tightly by the context and factors leading up to and within that moment. The context and inputs all change from moment to moment, and we therefore rarely see identical photos over and over again; this is the same for opinions, but these often masquerade as being much more representative and important.

Considering opinions as photos in this way is a useful technique to visualise the value of opinions. While they are certainly useful snapshots, it is impossible for them to be representative of something more innate or the 'way we are'. Actively recognising this in ourselves and others is extremely productive as it helps us treat opinions as useful transient outputs rather than something more fundamental, even though this is often how they feel. When we consider opinions in this transient way, we are able to more effectively understand their root causes, including relevant information, evidence, rationale and critical thinking. This can only result in better quality outcomes in the opinions themselves and the ability to communicate and reach common ground with others.

THE FALLACY OF A LACK OF CERTAINTY

The idea that not having absolute certainty (e.g. 99%) is the same as having no certainty (0%) is entirely false. This is evident when you start to think about it; for example, 80% certainty is significantly better than only 20%. However, it is crucial that we actively remind ourselves of this fact because our minds have a tendency, and weakness, to jump to easy or simplistic 'all or nothing' conclusions. It is much easier to make a snap judgement of 0% or 100% than challenging ourselves with the effort of thinking through nuance, complexity, and contraction to ultimately arrive at our own level of certainty of knowledge.

However, we absolutely can work out our level of certainty of knowledge or evidence, and in fact it is most important we do this when being tempted by the 0% or 100% tendency. If we are not actively aware, this tendency can cause us to make errors in our decisions, choices or actions.

This tendency to want to quickly get answers that are a yes or a no is similar to our bodies' desire and addiction to sugars and fats. We have an innate yearning to express that we have 0% or 100% certainty, and it feels good in the moment to do so. Similar to how we love to gorge on comfort foods, the inclination to express 0% or 100% certainty serves as a comfort zone for our minds, but can often be a common pitfall leading to negative outcomes.

Conversely, weighing up our level of certainty of knowledge of any particular thing or concept requires deliberate effort. This deliberate effort can include thinking, analysing or evaluating contradictory information, overlaying what we do not know, challenging our subjective bias, considering potential issues with the source information we are relying on or navigating opposite points of view.

Making a deliberate effort and avoiding this common trap is crucial to building and maintaining the strength of our minds. Actively building this into daily habits provides a robust and resilient foundation. We are unlikely to fall into this common trap when we understand it, can identify it and know how to challenge it.

It is important to remember that with many things, the fact that we cannot be 100% certain does not matter. For example, if you think it is 2 p.m. but only have 99% certainty, it is unlikely to be important. However, the more important a subject is, and the more it is driving a decision, choice or action, the more critical it is to be clear about your certainty level. This is why it is vital to be actively aware and seek to avoid the trap, regardless of our innate tendency to want to embrace the comforting fallacy that a lack of 100% knowledge or evidence is the same as 0% knowledge or evidence.

Ultimately, the more important the outcome, the more we should focus on working out our actual certainty levels. Making decisions, choices or actions based on a low certainty of knowledge is more likely to result in unintended consequences and an increased risk of negative outcomes.

EXERCISES

Exercise your mind by actively thinking through and wrestling with the key concepts from this chapter, including what is knowledge, how we create it, and what challenges do we have to ensure it is of the highest quality. Use the questions below to develop and boost your neural pathways. As with exercising your muscles, your mind will become stronger as you exercise it. Experiment with different ways of exercising and see which techniques work best for you:

- Explore in your mind – try it with your eyes closed or while doing physical exercise.
- Write your thoughts down, draw concepts or talk out loud to yourself.
- Work with others in dialogue.

Knowledge = Information + Experience + Intuition

- Play with these key concepts in your mind. Do you agree with the premise? If not, why not? If you do, why?
  1. Knowledge = Information + Experience + Intuition.
  2. There is no such thing as absolute certainty.
  3. The knowledge in our minds is on a spectrum of certainty, 0–99%, and this illustrates the central concept: that it is impossible to ever be 100% certain.
  4. Only you can work out the certainty level of each piece of knowledge in your mind.
- To challenge the central concept, are there any areas of knowledge

where you consider your certainty level to be 100%?

1. Where you have 100% certainty, what is the basis for this certainty level? Challenge yourself on why and your rationale. Consider what you would ask someone if they told you they had a 100% certainty level to find out why, and ask yourself the same questions.

2. Where you don't have a 100% certainty level, what are the types of things you would need to get closer to a 100% certainty level? Consider the section on critical thinking in Chapter 2 and Chapter 4's sections on the Dunning-Kruger effect and absolute certainty.

- Consider some examples of knowledge you have, such as an historical event, an opinion or a comment attributed to an individual, or a scientific theory:

    1. What is your immediate feeling of certainty level of for each piece of knowledge?

    2. Now, honestly self-reflect and analyse your actual level of certainty of the knowledge:

        - Consider the quality and veracity of the information, the nature of your experiences and your intuition.

        - Leverage critical thinking techniques.

        - Are there any differences in your certainty level compared to your initial immediate feelings and level of certainty?

- Think about examples of knowledge where you are reliant on information only (i.e. where you have minimal or no experience or even intuition):

    1. Do you consider any of this knowledge to have been created outside of your mind?

    2. If you do not have actual experiences related to creating the knowledge, do you think this reduces your certainty level of that knowledge?

    3. Where you are relying solely on information, have you considered how the information, or your perception of the

information, may be compromised?

4. Consider the intention or motivation of the source providing the information – could your information flow be distorted, or could your interpretation of information be filtered and warped by factors such as biases? Chapters 4 and 5 explore these potential issues in detail.

- Consider some examples of your knowledge for which it would be almost impossible to have experiences that could support it (e.g. landing on the moon):

    1. When you are stuck with only information and intuition, what would you need to do to increase your certainty level?

    2. Consider, given the increased importance of information and intuition, what is available to you to allow you to increase certainty levels. For example, you could consider critical thinking and tuning your mind's ear (Chapter 4).

    3. What would you hope you would do? Do you usually do this?

- Are you aware when you are using intuition in combination with information and experience? How important is it for determining your knowledge certainty level?

- Consider an example: assume information and experience are the same, but in one instance your intuition provides you high certainty and another low certainty. How much does intuition drive your overall certainty level, are you aware of this and what can you do to ensure it is at a level you want?

Chapter 4.
Tuning Your Mind's Ear

In our modern world, we are constantly bombarded with information. How we filter, interpret and process this information is subject to many challenges. If we are aware of these challenges, we can actively filter and control how we treat the information flowing into our minds, how we develop that information into knowledge and how we ensure our conclusions and actions are based on quality knowledge.

This chapter will help you become more consistently aware of these challenges. We will break the challenges down into their active ingredients and shine a light on the fingerprints they leave. There is a section exploring each one, so you can more easily identify it and understand how it is constructed. This will allow you to manage their impact on your information flow and minimise any potential distortion.

DUNNING-KRUGER EFFECT

The Dunning-Kruger effect explains why the less you know about a subject, the more likely you are to be blind to what you do not know. This makes you much more likely to think you have more expertise or knowledge than you actually do. Increasing your knowledge of a subject is like turning on the dimmer switch in a dark room; the more light there is, the more you realise how much there is in the room that you cannot fully see.

Dunning and Kruger identified the effect through their research on student exam self-assessments. Those who scored lowest ranked themselves much higher, while the highest performing underestimated their rankings.

Other examples we are likely to recognise from observations of others could include someone who is convinced they are a fantastic driver when in fact they are terrible. They are unaware of what a good driver would do, so don't know that they are not doing it. Another could be a celebrity who engages in political commentary while lacking a detailed knowledge of issues, but nevertheless states unwavering and forthright opinions.

While it is an important concept for us to understand within ourselves, it is also important that we recognise how the Dunning-Kruger effect can distort the information we receive from others into our minds. The information may have been modified because of the Dunning-Kruger effect, or it may exist entirely because of it. We need to be actively aware and consider whether the information we receive may have been subject to the Dunning-Kruger effect. We should always consider the extent to which the information may be affected, and therefore consider how much impact the Dunning-Kruger effect could have on the veracity, accuracy or bias of the information.

STRAWMANNING

The 'strawman' technique involves creating a distorted version, usually extreme and lacking nuance, of existing information, knowledge, opinion or conclusions. Information created as a result of strawmanning has been created specifically for the purpose of information distortion. Once the distortion is created, it is then used as a basis to argue against. Usually, the strawman distortion is created, deliberately or not, because it is easy to denigrate. This is because the distortion will have no nuance, and it presents a warped, extreme version of actual information, knowledge, opinion or conclusion.

For example, if someone said to you, 'I think it is crucial for your diet to contain plenty of vegetables and salads', you would be strawmanning their statement if you responded with, 'So you're saying we should just forget about burgers and eat nothing but leaves and twigs all day?'

Strawmanning can also be accidental or come about through ignorance because someone does not comprehend the actual information or knowledge, and has thus drawn flawed opinions or conclusions. This partial comprehension of the facts can then unknowingly lead to the creation of a distorted or oversimplified version of the information, knowledge, opinion or conclusion.

However, strawmanning is also done deliberately by some to undermine, obfuscate or advance an agenda. This deliberate use of strawmanning will usually misrepresent or discredit, stifle genuine discourse and promote hostility at the expense of seeking understanding or common ground.

Regardless of the intent, we should be aware that strawmanning is a common occurrence. Therefore, we should be aware that the information we are receiving may be affected by, or even the product of, strawmanning. Some of the common strawmanning distortions of information, knowledge, opinion or conclusion include:

- Oversimplification: drastically recreating a complex or layered fact pattern into a fake choice between only two options, e.g. yes or no, them or us, political x or political y, etc.

- Skewing focus: focusing on only one part of the information, knowledge, opinion or conclusion. This active ignoring of the numerous other factors is similar to oversimplification, and the effect is a misrepresenting of a tiny sliver of information as if that sliver were the whole thing.

- Out of context: the context is critical because if information, knowledge, opinions or conclusions are taken out of context, they no longer have meaning. Removing context is a huge distortion or transformation, and the strawman is an entirely new creation that has nothing to do with the actual information, knowledge, opinion or conclusion.

- Focusing on extremes: deliberately selecting a fringe or extreme element of the information, knowledge, opinion or conclusion to focus on and misrepresenting that fringe or extreme as being the whole.

ILLUSION OF POLARISATION

If we consider opinions on any subject on a sliding scale, it would appear that the vast majority of public debate is held from extreme ends. As a result, much of the information flowing into our minds is from these overwhelming extremes of the sliding scale, even though, in reality, the vast majority of opinions actually sit in the middle of the scale, similar to a bell curve distribution, as in Figure 5 below.

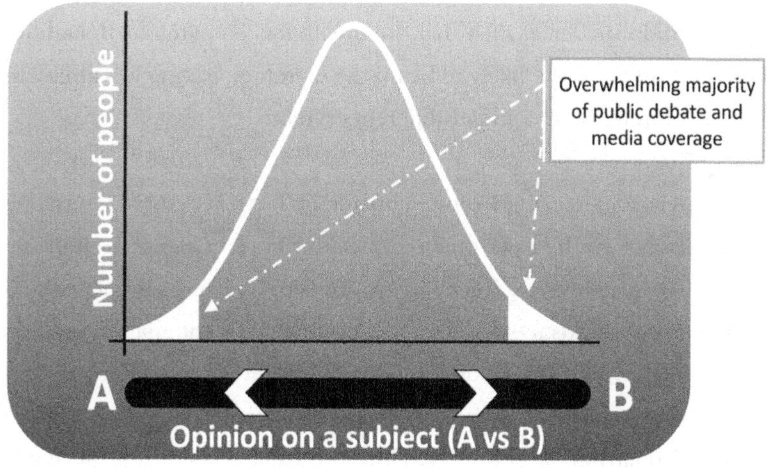

FIGURE 5

This illusion of polarisation is almost unavoidable; however, if we understand why it exists, we can filter the information that flows into our minds appropriately. The illusion of polarisation appears because of a predictable cyclical sequence:

1. Extreme opinions tend to lead to the strongest actions.

2. The strongest actions have the most impactful consequences.

3. The most impactful consequences are most prone to agitate and elicit response (in the short term).

4. The most extreme response will be from the most extreme opposite opinion.

5. This leads us to return to point 1.

By definition, any opinions in the middle will not register, although the middle of the bell curve contains the majority of people or opinions. Overlaying the Dunning-Kruger effect further exaggerates the illusion. That is, those with the most knowledge are aware of how much they do not know and are less likely to have a strong opinion. Those with more empathy or thoughtful consideration are also less likely to have a strong opinion, and vice versa, such that those with less empathy or thoughtful consideration are more likely to be on the extremes, having less ability to listen, comprehend or consider different opinions.

While this is not a recent phenomenon and, in fact, has existed for as long as our minds have had personality traits, our current use of technology significantly amplifies it. Technology not only actively stimulates and conditions our minds to seek out short-term reactive stimulation but also powers a highly effective feedback loop. This alchemy of technology and our inherent behaviours creates a compelling version of reality with an illusion of polarisation at its core. However, while this effect is inevitable and public debate will likely always tend to the extremes, we can correct the illusion by actively recognising it and acting to filter the information flowing into our minds as required.

NOT SEEING WHAT IS RIGHT IN FRONT OF US

Our minds are extremely powerful, constantly processing huge amounts of information and helping us prioritise focus for our conscious minds. However, this relentless prioritisation means we may sometimes not see what is right in front of us, whether that something is nefarious or not. The famous 'invisible gorilla' experiment is a demonstration of this concept and shines a light on some of the flaws in our minds. This includes our prioritisation, ability to focus on multiple things and our propensity to use mental shortcuts. In summary, when asked to watch a video and focus on counting an athlete's jumps, the majority of people do not notice a gorilla walking onto the screen because they are so focused on counting jumps. This poses the question to us all: how do we know this is not happening to us all the time? This is a useful question to help us strengthen our minds so that we can be alert to this possibility, develop awareness of our minds' weaknesses and work out strategies for mitigating it if it does happen.

How our minds prioritise and potentially miss things is subjective and a result of a complex combination of nature and nurture factors, including our neural plasticity, traits and intelligence. While this huge diversity of subjective prioritisation has obvious downsides, with some minds missing certain things and other minds being more vulnerable to missing things than others, this diversity also has a significant upside. That is, we, as a community, can learn and leverage from each other's perspectives on prioritisation. When we are aware of our minds' potential weaknesses, we can be on the lookout for when they may manifest.

INFORMATION BASED ON QUALITATIVE DATA

Not all information is created equal. Understanding differences in the quality of information is critical to enable us to understand the information. In particular, it is important to understand whether information flowing into our minds is based on qualitative data or evidence. Usually, non-numeric, qualitative data or evidence describes qualities or characteristics. In contrast to quantitative data, which is measured and expressed in numbers, qualitative data is generally gathered in discussions, interviews, observations or narrative surveys.

Qualitative data or evidence has inherent challenges compared to quantitative data in relation to its validity and reliability. For example, it is often based on subjective perception, which creates the potential for biases through the necessary interpretations. However, these challenges are often minimised or overlooked, and qualitative data is often erroneously awarded the same significance as quantitative data. This can lead to us unknowingly giving more credence to qualitative-based information than it deserves, which can result in the unintentional consequence of us developing knowledge in our minds that is based on information that lacks validity and reliability.

We should be actively aware of the increased risk of qualitative data or evidence leading to the creation of suboptimal knowledge in our minds. Awareness and active challenging will minimise the degradation of our information flow and reduce the likelihood of erroneous choices, decisions or actions resulting from that information flow.

Qualitative data and evidence can be important and are generally not intended to deceive. However, our lack of understanding and alertness to the potential weaknesses in qualitative data as an information source frequently leads to suboptimal knowledge creation and equally suboptimal consequences. Common instances of this include feedback being misinterpreted or extrapolated erroneously because of subjective interpretation and the assumed representativeness of the sample.

For example, a small group of people are interviewed about their opinion of their community and the results support a controversial point of view; however, no qualification of limits, representativeness or relevance of results is provided. Skewed perspectives or unrepresentative samples are critical factors that are easily obscured, deliberately or unwittingly. We also often see this in advertisements, with the very small print revealing a very low sample size relative to the actual or potential customer base. Rarely is any clarity provided on how the sample was selected – for example, was it from an existing group of loyal incentivised customers, or from a large random cross-section of society? The two results would likely be quite different.

Validity, reliability and generalisability are useful standards that can be applied to help us interpret the strength of qualitative data or evidence. Validity describes how precisely the data or evidence is reflected in the findings with respect to integrity and the application of relevant methodology. Reliability explains the consistency of the analytical procedures, while generalisability is crucial to understanding how much we should extrapolate the findings.

Validity, reliability and generalisability all exist on a sliding scale; however, the strength of each attribute for the relevant qualitative data or evidence is rarely clear. The lack of transparency around the shortcomings of qualitative information obscures our ability to understand the quality or veracity of the information, such as whether the information is based merely on a collection of individual opinions that could be subject to bias.

In addition to validity, reliability and generalisability, there are four other useful concepts to consider in understanding the quality of qualitative data or information. These are truth value, consistency, neutrality, and applicability, which are helpful concepts when considering the trustworthiness of interpretations, consistency of analyses, biases and the relevance of conclusions. All four methods seek to mitigate the issues with qualitative data or evidence. Truth value refers to the level of accuracy relative to the research topic, while consistency is about reliability and repeatability. Neutrality seeks to correct for bias in subjective interpretation, and applicability is the extent to which results can be extrapolated.

TAKING OFFENCE

Taking offence is an entirely subjective experience. Recognising that it is impossible to be offended unless we choose to be offended is an extremely important realisation.

Taking offence is something that happens only in our own minds, based on our own interpretations of the information we receive, and is influenced by a variety of factors. For example:

- Framing how the information is presented or contextualised. The way a statement is framed can influence how it is interpreted and what implications or meaning we attach to it.

- Projection of intent based on our own biases. We may assume that a statement is intended to be offensive based on our own experiences and beliefs.

- Assumptions in our interpretation. We may assume negative intentions or meaning behind a statement that might not exist because we do not have an understanding of the context or intent behind it.

- Vested interest affecting our sensitivity, particularly if we have a personal stake in potential outcomes.

- Personal insecurities can make us more prone to misinterpret comments or actions that are not actually intended as we interpreted them.

All of these factors contribute to the subjectivity in each of our minds, as our individual interpretations and reactions are influenced by our unique experiences and perceptions. What one person finds offensive, another may not, and vice versa.

Ultimately, taking offence is an entirely subjective experience that is extremely context specific and defined by personal interpretations, biases, assumptions and beliefs and individual vulnerabilities. It is important for us to be aware of and try to mitigate a disproportionate impact of these factors causing us, or others, to take offence. Mitigations include empathy, critical thinking and open-mindedness, which we should seek to be constantly harnessing.

CLAIMS OF ABSOLUTE CERTAINTY OF INFORMATION OR KNOWLEDGE

We should be wary of claims of absolute certainty of information or knowledge, not only because there is no such thing as absolute certainty (see Chapter 3) but also because these types of claims warrant additional scepticism. A claim of absolute certainty is a red flag that the information or knowledge being presented may be compromised, either unwittingly or deliberately, and perhaps nefariously.

The red flags from claims of certainty are even more relevant where distortion of information may be deliberate, such as when individuals or groups seek to manipulate others for their own purposes. This can include the spread of falsehoods and propaganda to sow confusion and doubt. When information is deliberately manipulated or distorted, it becomes difficult to discern the truth and to separate fact from fiction.

It is likely that all humans have, at some point, unwittingly passed on false or compromised information or knowledge. Well-intentioned minds may inadvertently alter information as it is recalled and communicated to others, either in person or using technology, leading to a loss of accuracy and reliability. Whether deliberate or unwitting, this will lead to distortion or alterations in knowledge and be amplified through the filters of interpretation, selective attention and groupthink.
Whether unwitting distortions or deliberate falsehoods, it is important to

approach claims of absolute certainty with scepticism. It is more likely that there is an intention, subconsciously or consciously deliberate, to manipulate and coerce choices, decisions or actions from others.

EXERCISES

Actively think through the two main concepts: firstly, that in our modern world we are subject to an endless deluge of information, much of which has issues that need filtering or treating. This is especially true if we are going to make choices, decisions or actions based on this information. Secondly, our minds are inherited from our ancestors and therefore are not always prepared to recognise and deal with these information issues.

Think deeply about the areas discussed and reflect on the questions below to develop and boost your neural pathways. Explore each of the main information issues so you can more easily identify them and understand how they work and how they can be avoided or managed. This should help minimise any potential distortion on your information flow. Experiment with different ways of exercising and see which techniques work best for you:

- Explore in your mind – try it with your eyes closed or while doing physical exercise.
- Write down your thoughts, draw concepts or talk out loud to yourself.
- Work with others in dialogue.

Dunning-Kruger Effect

- Think about examples of the Dunning-Kruger effect, whether in public debate, politics, literature or film, or where you have observed the effect directly in your own interpersonal experiences.

What are the steps that would have been required to minimise the effect?

- Self-reflect on examples where you have exhibited the effect yourself – how could you be more self-aware of these situations or contexts in real time?
- Think about the examples that you have in your mind now and be really honest:
  1. Are there things you don't actually know much about, but you think you do?
  2. Reflect on where you currently do this and consider how much impact there has been on the veracity, accuracy or bias of information you have used or have provided to others.
  3. What can you do to minimise this tendency in your mind? For example, closely monitor when you think you're utterly right, and are emotionally involved with that sense of certainty about a subject, but deep down you know this is probably unjustified.
- Practise active awareness and consideration of whether the information you receive from others may have been subject to the Dunning-Kruger effect:
  1. Seek to understand and analyse the extent to which the information you receive may be affected and what you need to do to correct for its effects.
  2. Certain types of information are more likely to be at risk, for example based on the characteristics of the sender, the type of information or whether the information seeks to drive an outcome.

Strawmanning

- Reflect on when you have been aware of strawmanning:
  1. What were the features? For example, was the context accidental,

through ignorance or deliberate?

2. How did the distortion or oversimplification of the information, knowledge, opinion or conclusion work?

3. Do you think it was deliberate and intended to undermine, obfuscate or advance an agenda?

- Practise building awareness through observation, such as watching the news or observing conversations between others and considering the following:

  1. Note how common it is that neither party is aware.

  2. Could you develop an awareness of the indicators or red flags?

  3. What do you think you need to monitor or look out for so you can see it happening in your own interactions, whether by yourself or by others?

- Practise creating strawmans through your own misrepresentations. Do this in your mind, on your own and with others. This will help you familiarise yourself with the methods of creation and what different types of strawmen look like. Building your strawmanning capability will significantly increase your ability to recognise strawmen created by others.

- Think about how your information flow may be affected by, or even the product of, strawmanning.

- Consider how you would detect the following common distortions in your information flow (these terms are explained in the main chapter section on strawmanning):

  1. oversimplification

  2. skewing focus

  3. out of context

  4. focusing on extremes

- Once you know how to identify a strawman, it can be very helpful to point them out to others since many are created accidentally; even if they are created deliberately, a common understanding of the strawman can usually help all parties move beyond it.

- Here are the key steps to identify a strawman and the differences in the original information, knowledge, opinion or conclusions:

  1. Identify the key points in the strawman – that is, the key points in how the strawman argument is constructed and, more importantly, how they are different from the original information, knowledge, opinion or conclusion. Drawing the line between the original and the strawman makes it explicit where the divergence sits.

  2. Invest as much time as is needed to clarify the original information, knowledge, opinion or conclusion. Often, the strawman is created unintentionally because of a lack of alignment on the actual underlying information or knowledge.

  3. Be very specific in calling out the key elements of what has been misrepresented or even what has been omitted.

  4. Explain and seek agreement on how the misrepresentation or omissions create distortions from the original information, knowledge, opinion or conclusion.

  5. Once aligned, agree to put the strawman behind you and focus on the common ground you have developed. Dwelling on an old strawman is extremely unproductive.

Illusion of Polarisation

- Familiarise yourself with the bell curve (Figure 5). Does it make sense to you, and do you agree there is an illusion of polarisation?

- Think about some subjects you know well. Do you recognise the way extreme polarised opinions disproportionately dominate public debate?

- Think about some examples where this effect is particularly pronounced and validate your assumptions with others.

- Consider whether someone who is neutral on a topic is likely to proclaim their neutrality loudly?

- Modern technology has provided us with a virtual town square for discussion. Think about how this analogy plays out in a real town square. Do you recognise a characterisation that a few people are shouting loudly while most people are elsewhere in the town, at home relaxing or acquiring information and experiences for themselves?

- Imagine being on one extreme of the bell curve – how likely do you think you would be to be empathetic to those on the opposite extreme?

- Imagine you understand both extremes really well – are you likely to have a nuanced opinion, hold a balanced point of view or express a neutral perspective?

- Consider how extreme your opinion is likely to be if you know there is much that you do not know – do you think this would increase the likelihood of a humble sensibility? Consider an analogy – how careful would someone be, and how delicately would they approach the task, disarming a bomb if they knew there were many unknown variables compared to one big simple button?

- Think about why it is important for media and social media companies to embrace the effect of an illusion of polarisation:
  1. To what extent does it drive a significant benefit to their business model?
  2. In a business model where eyeball hours are everything, is your attention more likely to be drawn by dramatic sensationalism or neutral, non-committal content?

- Think about the extent to which you want sensationalist information. How much are you stimulated by hero and villain representation versus balanced nuance?
  1. How can you apply this understanding to your day-to-day information flow? For example, how much is your attention consumed by the edges of the bell curve versus the middle?

- Consider how inevitable you think the illusion of polarisation is and how you can adjust how you process your information flow accordingly:

1. Consider the reality of the bell curve. If the overwhelming majority of opinions are in the middle, what does that mean about the reality you perceive? Challenge yourself to evaluate the illusion of polarisation compared to reality and use it to help guide your perspective.

- Ask yourself, given the bell curve, who are all the other people, and where are their voices? Can you seek them out, and how much do you think they are encouraged to conform to the edge of the bell curve when, in fact, they are in the middle?

Not Seeing What Is Right in Front of Us

- Consider how you prioritise your focus in your day-to-day activities – what could you be missing as a result of this prioritisation?
- Watch the 'invisible gorilla' video online.
- Watch it a second time, but try to be actively self-aware of what you are doing differently:
  1. Reflect on what you are doing that is the same and what is different.
  2. Can you apply lessons learned more broadly in your daily life?
- Consider if you can be more actively aware of how your mind tends to prioritise, including how subjective it is and what impact your neural plasticity, traits and intelligence have on this prioritisation.
- Which contexts, subjects, interactions with others and your own thinking are more likely to be disproportionately impacted by your prioritisation?

Information Based on Qualitative Data

- Think about some examples of topics you know well where information is mainly qualitative data or evidence:
  1. Do you recognise the challenges with qualitative versus

quantitative data or evidence?

2. Consider what these challenges mean for the veracity of the knowledge you are creating based on this information.

3. Consider whether a decision, choice or action is being driven by this information. Is there a higher bar for qualitative data or evidence? Should there be?

- Experiment with applying the below considerations to some examples of information based on qualitative data – this can help determine the strength of the information:

1. Accounting for subjective biases, including subjective interpretation of data and any conclusions, are there consistent and transparent interpretations, and is it clear that there has been sufficient objectivity and challenge?

2. Were the input questions of appropriate granularity, and was the depth of narrative descriptions sufficient to justify the outputs?

3. Is it clear that there were no biases in sampling?

4. Is it clear that the critical analysis was appropriate in terms of depth, breadth and relevance of data to ensure no perspectives were inappropriately excluded?

5. When data or evidence was provided directly from interviewees, how accurately was it captured, and how accurate are the relevant conclusions drawn from it?

6. What was the extent of repetition and changing of variables to substantiate findings? For example, were multiple datasets and multivariant analyses used to substantiate the result, and at the very least to minimise correlation being interpreted as causation?

7. How rigorous and consistent was the end-to-end process from data gathering to interpretation and drawing conclusions? Is there any independent assurance of this process?

Taking Offence

- Think about some examples of when you have been offended. Include trivial and profound examples, together with those that were accidental and also deliberate. For each example, consider:
  1. Was it helpful taking offence?
  2. What happened as a result of you taking offence – did it change anything?
  3. Could you have chosen not to take offence in any of the examples?
  4. When is choosing to take offence not within your control?
  5. When would taking offence be a priority over using your energy on constructive and pleasurable activities for you?
- Consider some examples of people who claim to have taken offence and think about the specific situations and contexts. With this in mind, are there any exceptions to the idea that taking offence is an entirely subjective experience, where everything and nothing can be offensive? What are these exceptions and how can you be aware of and manage them?
- Taking offence is usually the result of multiple factors, even if it is expressed as one outcome, but it is usually difficult to understand which factor is more or less responsible for the outcome. We can therefore use these techniques to help determine the main root cause:
  1. Empathise with the person who has taken offence to understand their perspective.
  2. Apply critical thinking to objectively analyse the situation and context.

Claims of Absolute Certainty of Information or Knowledge

- Think about some examples of claims of absolute certainly of information or knowledge. Challenge yourself – do you have any that you subscribe to? – and consider the following:
  1. On what basis are they formed?
  2. What is the actual certainty level – why is it characterised as absolute?
  3. Does the 'absolute' nature directly drive choices, decisions or actions?
  4. Is the 'absolute' unwitting or symptomatic of deliberate distortions or falsehoods?
  5. Think about why it is a claim of absolute certainty. What is the need for such an exaggerated claim? Is it an unwitting distortion or deliberate? If it is deliberate, why?
- Think about claims of absolute certainty that you know of that affect others:
  1. How is the certainty conveyed and the support for the claim enforced?
  2. How is interrogation or investigation of the claim of certainty muted, how are others convinced and how are their choices, decisions or actions coerced?

Reflect on why it is important to approach claims of absolute certainty with scepticism, whether they are unwitting distortions or deliberate falsehoods – consider that it is more likely that there is an intention, subconsciously or consciously deliberate, to manipulate and coerce choices, decisions or actions from others.

Chapter 5.
The Problem with Words

Knowledge, concepts and their meanings exist in our minds across the vast complexity of our neural networks. Typically, we have over one hundred billion neurons interconnected by up to a thousand trillion synapses in our neural network. This huge complexity renders the perfect transfer of even a small amount of knowledge or concepts from one mind to another incredibly challenging.

To tackle this challenge, we rely heavily on words. In many ways, words are the method we use to categorise, define and colour our knowledge and concepts. The ability to linguistically map what is in our minds has undoubtedly been a significant differentiator, enabling us to thrive as a species. However, this linguistic mapping capability is subject to certain weaknesses that we can be aware of and correct to some extent. We'll explore this further in this chapter.

Words, especially in small quantities, can only bluntly convey the complexity of the knowledge or concepts we hope to transfer between our minds. The usual transfer quality from one mind to another using words alone is often low. We often seek to supplement words with body language or intonation, which certainly enhances the quality of communication, but significant barriers remain. The enormous complexity of what exists in one mind is challenging to capture in words, which are subject to the distortions of both the receiver and sender of information in the form of biases, assumptions, inferences and expectations.

Music, for example, can be a significantly more effective communication tool, especially when communicating emotion and conceptual thought. However, despite all the shortcomings of words as a communication tool, they remain our best available general-purpose tool. We should, therefore, be alert to the potential issues and seek to proactively mitigate risks to ensure we communicate as effectively as possible.

FINDING OUR WORDS

The process of creating knowledge or concepts in our minds and then converting them into words is imperfect at best. We boil down and reduce the knowledge or meaning until we find the words that most closely align with it. Knowledge or concepts are boundaryless, expansive, dynamic and transient in our minds. To convert this rich complexity of thought into words, we condense ruthlessly, creating a simplified and reduced essence of our thoughts while seeking words that best approximate this residual meaning.

This process, driven by the need to export our thoughts, heavily relies on our subjective interpretation of what words mean. This interpretation is important, but equally important is how we map this meaning to our thoughts. In general, we incorrectly assume that converting our thoughts into words is a two-way process. We assume that when we convert thoughts to words, those words can be perfectly converted back to the same thoughts by another mind. Additionally, we believe we can recreate thoughts from another mind by converting their words into our own thoughts.

However, when complex thoughts are distilled into words, there is typically a reduction in the sophistication of those thoughts. This reduction occurs because words are allocated based on a best fit for the residual meaning. As a result, the words usually cannot represent the full original meaning or knowledge.

The error when converting words to knowledge and back again can be negligible or enormous. The more complex the original thought, the higher the probability of error. For example, a simple statement like 'I'm hungry' is less prone to error than explaining a multifaceted political opinion, which involves a more complex thought process and is, therefore, more susceptible to errors when translated into words and back into thoughts in another person's mind.

The significant amount of 'noise' this transfer process is subject to is shown in Figure 6 below, which illustrates that meaning or knowledge is lost or distorted in each step of the transfer. The transfer quality is significantly better in example 3 than in example 1, which is subject to less noise and distortion in the transfer process. Less noise could be due to many factors, including clarity of context, using more words, qualifying definitions, being specific, explaining why, clarification through true back-and-forth dialogue, and validation.

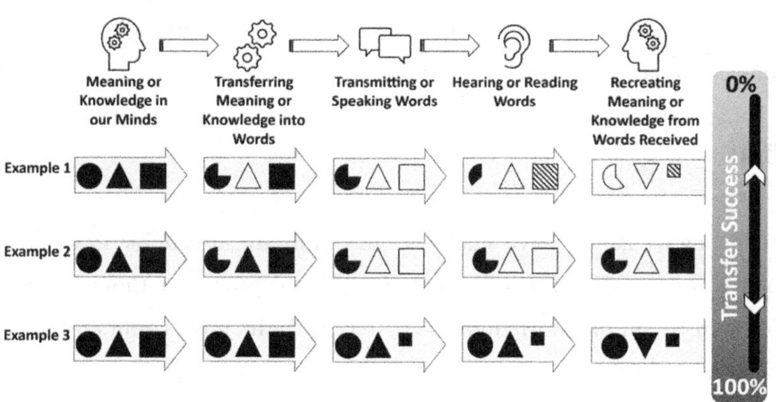

FIGURE 6

While we are generally aware of these challenges – for example, when we say, 'words just can't describe it' – we tend not to embrace the fact that words can never fully convey the depth and complexity of what we have in our minds. Even if we had infinite words and time, it would remain effectively impossible. However, understanding these inherent limitations in our minds allows us to try to minimise errors and noise in our communications. A critical aspect in this endeavour is to never assume that the words you create precisely match your thoughts and that the words you receive from others exactly represent their thoughts. Instead, seek to constantly provide context and clarification, whether you are transmitting or receiving.

BEYOND OUR BIASES

Biases, assumptions, inferences, expectations and mapping shortcuts, are the main causes of error and noise in our communications. These filters are all innate in our minds, and while they are not as essential to us as they were to our ancestors, they continue to be useful in our modern world. However, if they are not monitored in the context of our communication with others, they can have a corrosive effect on our ability to transfer knowledge or meaning from one mind to another.

Bias

Following us like our own shadows, our minds are susceptible to various biases. These affect how we create words to capture our thoughts and our perception of information being received, the most common biases included:

- *Confirmation bias* is when we give precedence to the elements or interpretations of what we hear that align with what we are predisposed to hear, whether consciously or subconsciously. This creates a situation where existing knowledge in our minds is disproportionately bolstered by what we hear, and contradictions to our existing knowledge are disproportionately dismissed. This causes us to retain incorrect knowledge and even falsehoods. The impact is also pervasive in driving our actions, as we selectively search for, interpret or recall information that confirms our pre-existing knowledge while ignoring or discounting information that contradicts it.

- *Halo effect bias* is our mind's tendency to form an overall impression of something based on a single positive or negative element. The effect can also work in reverse; for example, if we encounter a person, object or idea with a negative element, we might form a negative impression of it as a whole and actively disregard potentially positive elements. Overall, the halo effect bias can lead us to interpret information or knowledge inaccurately, reducing our objectivity and increasing the likelihood of deliberately disregarding available information.

- *Framing effect bias* is when our minds are susceptible to the way information is presented and how this influences our interpretation of its meaning. This can significantly impact the way we perceive the risks and benefits of the information. A good example is to consider two options: option 1 is presented as a '90% chance of survival', while option 2 is presented as a '10% chance of death'. Without any bias, the two options are essentially the same. However, because of the framing of option 1 in a positive light and option 2 more negatively, our minds are inherently drawn to perceiving the options as different; this is the framing effect bias.

We should be alert to others seeking to take advantage of this bias in our minds through propaganda or advertising. However, it is also inevitable that most information will be framed in some way or another, often with no deliberate or nefarious intentions. This is why it is important to recognise the framing effect bias and base our interpretations on rational or objective information rather than how it is presented. We can also bolster this approach by seeking out information from multiple sources and considering information from a neutral perspective.

- *Availability bias* refers to a tendency for our minds to rely on information that is easily accessible or memorable, even if it is not representative of the wider context or specific situation. Essentially, the more easily we can recall or access information, the more likely we will use it as a basis for our decisions and judgements. Our minds do this routinely, relying on recent news stories or personal experiences to inform our interpretation of information, even if they are not representative of the wider context. We often go further still by ignoring other important factors or information that is less readily available or memorable.

Being aware of our tendency for this bias and making interventions to consider all available information, while avoiding reliance solely on what is easily accessible or memorable, can help mitigate the effects of the availability bias. Additionally, seeking out a range of perspectives and sources of information is an important rule of thumb, together with investing sufficient time to evaluate information based on its actual relevance. These methods should help minimise, or at least help us be aware of, any disproportionate reliance we are placing on information that is not truly representative.

- *Anchoring bias* is how our minds tend to give more weight to the first piece of information we receive, regardless of its accuracy or relevance, and use it as a reference point to make subsequent judgements or decisions. Our minds create a sort of mental 'anchor' that can be difficult to shift, even when presented with contradictory evidence. This can lead to biased judgements and decisions that are not based on a full and accurate understanding or knowledge.

- *Recency bias* is our predisposition to give more weight to information or knowledge that is more recent in our minds, regardless of whether the information or knowledge is more relevant or accurate. This can lead to errors in interpretation, since it causes us to overlook or discount important information simply because it is not fresh in our minds. When we focus solely on the most recent information we have encountered, we may overlook important concepts or forget key details from earlier learning experiences. This can make our understanding and interpretations flawed, leading to a shallow or surface-level understanding of complex subjects and the creation of low-quality knowledge in our minds. We can actively counteract the recency bias through awareness by intentionally seeking out and considering earlier information.

These biases are inherent in all our minds; we inherited them from our ancestors, and they were crucial to their survival, enabling rapid decision-making with minimal cognitive effort. However, it is important to actively engage in critical thinking and consider alternative perspectives to mitigate the negative effects of these biases in our modern world. This involves being aware of the biases in our minds and actively seeking out and considering differing viewpoints. We should also actively consider how the biases manifest in others' minds and how that may impact the information we receive and process.

Our minds have their own set of biases operating constantly, to a greater or lesser extent. When we actively challenge how our minds process and interpret information, together with an acute awareness of all these biases, we can mitigate their effects. As we analyse information and evaluate it objectively, rather than relying solely on our personal biases, we should seek out diverse sources of information and perspectives. This will help us broaden our understanding and improve our ability to listen and interpret information accurately and objectively.

Assumptions

Our minds actively use assumptions as a useful tool to navigate our lives more efficiently. We create and quickly update a subjective set of assumptions – many justified and many not. We have an innate preference to favour evidence that matches our assumptions. Our ancestors would have significantly benefited from this as it allows for more rapid decision-making in the short term. However, as we know, assumptions can also be false. The nature of our reliance on them as shortcuts for quick decision-making increases the likelihood of error in the quality of our interpretation and decision-making, ultimately resulting in distorted knowledge or concepts. This risk is amplified for complex concepts, but even simple words like 'global warming' or 'red meat' can be subject to assumed literal meanings by some.

Regardless of the genesis of our assumptions, they can be a significant weakness in our ability to communicate coherently, so we should seek to actively validate them as being correct within the context they are being applied.

Inference

Our minds tend to jump to conclusions, inferring a conclusion where it is not necessarily justified. This happens most often when correlation is inferred as causation. For example, Japanese people have a diet of Japanese food, and the Japanese have a population crisis. Therefore, Japanese food causes population crises.

Just because two facts correlate does not mean that one causes the other. In fact, assuming causation between correlated events causes us to develop false knowledge in our minds and drives incorrect and even dangerous choices, decision-making and actions.

In addition to an incorrect inference of causation from correlation, we are also prone to another type of error known as logical inference – for example, the assumption that eagles can fly, and eagles are birds; therefore, all birds can fly.

Both types of inference errors are common because our minds are inherently predisposed to seek out patterns even if they do not exist. We previously explored this idea in the section on 'mind cravings' inherited from our ancestors. While our predisposition to seek patterns is an important skill, and was no doubt an extremely important capability in our survival historically, in our modern world it results in side effects that we should be aware of and manage. We can largely eliminate its effects by being aware of the tendency and making simple interventions, such as challenging the rationale for conclusions of causation based only on a simple univariant correlation.

Expectations

Our minds are immensely powerful in framing our experience in the context that we are expecting. So, if we think we will enjoy an experience, we are more likely to enjoy it, as opposed to negative expectations of an experience making it less likely that we will enjoy it. Our minds' projection of expectation is enormously powerful. It can manifest in real physical effects, such as the placebo and nocebo effects, and we see this being exploited every day in illusions, manipulations and scams.

Ultimately, the expectations in our minds result from our conditioning and how our neural pathways, concerning our neuroplasticity, have been developed. Similar to assumptions, expectations are a significant weakness in our ability to coherently understand the words we hear unless they are validated as correct within the context in which they are being applied.

Mapping Shortcuts

Over time, we build 'mappings' in our minds, which are shortcuts to efficiently arrive at conclusions of knowledge or meaning. While these shortcuts can be useful, they are all vulnerable to our biases, assumptions, inferences and expectation errors and, therefore, require constant monitoring and challenge to minimise the risk of making incorrect interpretations and actions as a result. We should actively challenge our minds to be consciously aware that we are relying on a 'mapping' and consider the overall benefit of the shortcut compared to the potential downsides.

Words Without Context

A word cannot exist without context. However, in our modern world, there is an increasing infantilisation of language, where certain words are assumed to carry a weight of meaning regardless of context or even with no context at all. We must provide full context to our words to ensure we are truly communicating what is in our minds and to prevent it being lost in others' assumptions, expectations or biases.

We all know of examples where one word can have two or more completely different meanings, such as bat as a mammal and sports equipment, bank as a financial institution and side of a river, or bark from a tree or a dog. While these may seem trivial or obviously not at risk of creating confusion, if you really consider them, without specific context being made clear it is impossible to know the actual intended meaning. This is the same for all words. The more complex the topic, or context, the more important this becomes. This is because our minds associate significant amounts of information with words, but this association only exists in our minds. We therefore need to explain very clearly what the words we are using mean to us and anticipate that they will likely mean something different to the receiver of those words. Generally, a good amount of meaning can be conveyed through appropriate context setting and careful consideration to explain any meaning associated with the word that the receiver may not have, which needs to be anticipated. When we make assumptions as a sender or receiver of words, we significantly increase the risk of miscommunication and the likelihood of a 'trigger word' response. This also acts to minimise any nefarious, or inadvertent, tendencies to remove context and apply pre-made conclusions that a 'word without context' invites.

TRANSMITTING AND RECEIVING WORDS

Transmission

Transmitting words through speech is subject to significant noise and error. We hope the words we say are received exactly as we deliver them. We expect that our intent in speaking is conveyed the way we intend. However, this is unlikely due to the plethora of variations in how we say words – tone, articulation, emphasis, body language, eye contact, nuance, situational context, relationship context, language or dialect. The non-verbal elements of this communication tend to be most relevant when conveying emotions, attitudes or certain nuances; for example, a frown, smile or wink can convey what might be quite difficult verbally. However, when it comes to transmitting complex information, sharing ideas or expressing abstract concepts, verbal communication is far superior, despite the many challenges.

Spoken words suffer these challenges; however, written words suffer from these and additional challenges. Written words have a weakness in their lack of context. Written words can suffer from imperfect transfer without instant feedback, or the variations used in how spoken words are transmitted. This includes the risk of nuance, context and meaning being lost. While it is a challenge to perfectly communicate words from one mind to another, our minds have many techniques to reduce the noise and error rate. These include:

- being specific
- explaining why
- playing back what you have understood
- asking others to play back what they have understood
- seeking precision
- qualifying definitions

Receiving Words and Converting them into Knowledge and Meaning

Before the sound waves of a word vibrate our eardrums or our optic nerve is stimulated by photons, our minds apply assumptions, filters and judgements. As we hear or read words, we actively update these assumptions, filters and judgements based on tone, articulation, emphasis, body language, eye contact, nuance, situational context, relationship context, language or dialect.

The resultant landing of words in our minds is a product of all these factors, which we process in real time and overlay with our interpretations, as explored in 'Beyond Our Biases', to convert the words into knowledge or concepts. Such a complex and subjective multitude of factors occurring in real time means that the transfer of what is in one mind to another is highly likely to be imperfect, as illustrated in Figure 6.

Despite these challenges, words and verbal in-person communication continue to be the best tools and systems available to us, and they are effective, given the huge complexity of concepts and knowledge in our minds. However, we can seek to minimise the noise in the transfer process by being actively aware of the most likely causes of disruption and seeking to mitigate these challenges using the conscious elements of our minds.

At the same time, it is important to recognise that the subconscious elements of our minds are responsible for a significant amount of our mind activity during communication and cause much of the noise highlighted above. While we cannot directly control our subconscious, we can influence it over time by being aware of and acting to correct for issues such as bias, assumptions, expectation, inference and mapping shortcuts. Awareness and proactive action in our listening and interpretation, as we convert the words we hear to knowledge or concepts, is also essential to ensure effective communication of the meaning or knowledge from one mind to another.

EXERCISES

Focus your mind on trying to comprehend the challenge of transferring the enormous complexity of thoughts from one mind to another mind, completely and without any distortion. Then consider that we primarily rely on words for this transfer process, and how prone words are to error for both the sender and receiver.

Against this backdrop, tackle the exercises below by deeply inspecting how your assumptions, biases, inferences and expectations effect your communication, both as a sender and a receiver of information. Experiment with different ways of exercising your mind and creating new pathways to determine which techniques work best for you:

- Explore in your mind – try it with your eyes closed or while doing physical exercise.
- Write down your thoughts, draw concepts or talk out loud to yourself.
- Work with others in dialogue.

Finding Our Words

- Think about the process of converting knowledge and meaning into words in your mind. Create some examples to use in these exercises, considering both simple and complex thoughts together with conceptual and emotional ideas:

1. Write down the thoughts as words, then try to objectively read them as if they were someone else's words, ignoring your original intent as much as you can. Now consider how content are you with the words and how accurately they capture your intended knowledge and meaning.

- Think through the inherent limitations that create so much noise in the communication from one mind to another, considering Figure 6:

1. Do you recognise the stages of transmission – are these stages fixed or do they change depending on context? Think through different contexts and how each affects the likelihood of error.

2. Do you recognise the potential noise issues at each stage, and the impact on transmission quality at each stage?

- Given that the words you create will never be an exact match of your thoughts, or that the words you receive from others will never be an exact match of their thoughts:

1. What can you do to minimise noise?

2. What can you do to help ensure you have the most effective communication?

3. How can you use the tools you do have to provide you with the highest chance of successful communication? Consider articulation, emphasis, body language, eye contact, nuance, situational context, relationship context, language or dialect.

4. How often do you check back, asking the other person to explain what they have understood to confirm that what you have said has been understood correctly? And how often do you do the reverse and validate that you have understood what someone else is saying? Can you do this more often and more consistently?

Biases

- Think about an example of each type of bias that you have seen used by others (refer to the main chapter for definitions):
    1. confirmation
    2. halo
    3. framing
    4. availability
    5. anchoring
    6. recency
- Was the bias deliberate?
- What techniques could others use to be more self-aware when they inadvertently demonstrate bias?
- Now consider if any of these techniques would be useful for you to use in your self-awareness of your biases. Are there any additional biases that you employ, and how can you be aware of them and manage their impact?

Assumptions

- Are you actively aware of when you make assumptions?
    1. Try to be as objective as possible and analyse some examples, including interactions with others or through other sources of your information flow.
    2. We rightly rely heavily on assumptions as shortcuts; however, they are not always correct, and we should be actively aware of when we are making assumptions so we can challenge and identify contexts where the assumptions are not, in fact, correct.
- Actively consider these questions to provide a basis for and help validate your assumptions:

1. Is the assumption based on well-understood data or evidence?

2. Do you understand all the relevant building blocks for the assumption and how those building blocks interact?

3. Is there a risk you are blinkered by limiting your focus to only selected inputs and outputs? Consider if you are understanding things as a 'black box' rather than the complexity within.

4. Is the assumption based on a desire to eliminate any grey area or ambiguity rather than consider the actual complexity or nuance?

5. Have you considered the risk that the assumption relies on correlation as being indicative of causation?

Inference

*   Consider our example of 'Japanese people overwhelmingly have a diet of Japanese food, and Japan has a population crisis; therefore, Japanese food causes population crises'. Why is this wrong, and how do you identify that it is wrong?

1. Think through where you have seen other obvious examples of correlation being taken as causation.

2. Try to create your own examples of deliberate inference errors, both correlation and logical inference. As you do this, think about how you do this and the 'fingerprints' that are left behind that you will recognise in the future.

3. Think about the steps you can take to minimise the risk of making these inference errors yourself, and also how you would identify and correct information with inference errors you receive from others.

Expectations

- Practise being actively aware of a situation, being alert to when you are applying expectations before you have received words and while you are hearing and processing words:
  1. Try replaying the situation afterwards in your mind. Does ignoring your expectations change the outcome?
  2. Now, try and imagine the situation but in a different context. How would the context change your expectations and the outcome?
- Self-reflect on different examples across a range of interactions or information flows. For each, consider how your expectations were created and how they helped or contributed to errors in transmission:
  1. Think about the best method for you to use to be aware of how you form your expectations. How dependent is it on context and how much can it change your interpretation?
  2. Consider how you can validate your expectations within the context that they are being applied, before they can cause errors in transmission.

Mapping Shortcuts

- Reflect on the concept of mapping shortcuts and consider some examples of application in your decision-making process. For instance, think about interactions with familiar individuals or navigating familiar roads that enable quicker problem-solving:
  1. While many of these mapping shortcuts are useful and help us work things out more efficiently, think about where they may be vulnerable to your biases, assumptions, inferences and expectation errors in your decision-making process.
  2. Consider where you see others taking mapping shortcuts that have potential downsides – for example, where they lead to

misplaced trust, risky guesses or misinterpretations.

3. Reflect on your own mapping shortcuts and identify any potential downsides that might outweigh the perceived benefit of using these shortcuts, such as less time or less effort.

4. Think about how you can be more aware of your mapping shortcuts and how you can monitor and challenge them. This should minimise the risk of the shortcut causing less optimal outcomes than would be achieved without the shortcut – in other words, the shortcut is not causing more harm than good.

Words Without Context

- Can you think of examples of words that exist without context?
  1. Consider how meaning can be created from a word without context. What are the assumptions, expectations and biases that need to be applied, and where do these come from?
  2. Are you content that you seek sufficient context, or are you comfortable to draw conclusions with minimal or no context based on your assumptions, expectations and biases?
  3. Think about what you need from interactions with others or your information flow to provide sufficient context:
     - Do you consistently seek to provide the same context to others?
     - Without this, do you think you are truly communicating what is in your mind? Are you comfortable there is no risk it is being lost in others' assumptions, expectations or biases?

Chapter 6.
Optimising Overall Mind Health

Maintaining good mind health is important regardless of the strength of your mind. Similar to our physical health, neglecting it can diminish even the strongest minds. In this chapter, we will look at the factors that contribute to maintaining good mind health.

SLEEP

Sleep deprivation is linked to a lengthy list of physical and mind issues affecting virtually every aspect of our lives. Ensuring you have high-quality and sufficient sleep is essential for the health and strength of your mind, so you should prioritise and make time for a healthy amount of sleep.

Slow-wave (SW) sleep, and the more well-known rapid eye movement (REM) sleep, are two important stages of our sleep cycle. During SW sleep, our brainwaves slow down, with our body deeply relaxing. This deep sleep is important for physical restoration and recovery, such as repairing tissues, boosting the immune system and releasing growth hormones.

While in REM sleep, the brain becomes more active, and we experience vivid dreams. REM sleep is crucial for emotional processing, memory consolidation and learning. Both SW and REM sleep are critical for mind health and strength. Multiple stages of these sleep cycles characterise healthy sleep throughout each night. Each stage serves different functions, and the deprivation or disruption of our sleep cycle usually has negative consequences for our mind health – and our physical health, too.

SPIRAL UP, SPIRAL DOWN

Our minds are predisposed not to appreciate how good we have it when we are 'up' and, conversely, to feel we will never get back 'up' when we are 'down'. Understanding this tendency is important so we can moderate how much this predisposition affects our mind health and strength. Secondary effects also magnify both the positive and negative impacts of this tendency. Your choices and actions can interact in a cycle that can spiral upwards or downwards. For example, if you are anxious or depressed, your negative thoughts may lead to behaviours like social withdrawal or reduced general activity. These behaviours can reinforce negative thoughts and feelings in a self-fulfilling downward spiral. When in a downward spiral, you are more likely to overlook opportunities to improve yourself as you perceive them pessimistically. Conversely, you can start a positive cycle towards recovery by recognising and changing your negative thoughts, engaging in positive behaviours and cultivating positive emotions.

YOUR PERSPECTIVE

Perspective is one of the most important tools you can use to adjust your outlook and improve your mind health and strength. Altering your perspective can help address many of your perceived shortcomings, such as your predisposition to fear or taking things for granted. Maximising the benefits you can gain from your actions is also hugely important. For example, your ability to derive satisfaction from the efforts you invest in hard work allows you to find purpose beyond the practical aspects of the work.

Changing your perspective can profoundly impact your mind health and strength. Often, our thoughts and beliefs can become stuck in negative patterns that fuel feelings of anxiety, depression and low self-esteem. However, we have the power to break free and escape from these negative patterns by taking control of our minds and intentionally changing our perspective. While it can seem daunting to do this at first, with practice it gets easier and we are able to do it more quickly. A good place to start with changing your perspective is through 'reframing'. For example, if you notice negative thoughts creeping in, you can attempt to reframe them more positively. So, instead of saying, 'I'm never going to be able to do this', reframe it as, 'I might struggle at first, but with practice, I will get better.'

We can also challenge our self-knowledge. For example, many of us have deeply ingrained beliefs that actively hold us back, such as, 'I'm not smart enough' or 'I'm not worthy of love.' We should actively monitor ourselves for these beliefs and challenge them in the same way we challenge external information and knowledge.

Practising gratitude and seeking out new experiences are also highly effective ways of altering our perspectives. See 'Practising gratitude and generosity' in the activities section of this chapter.

LOVE

Love can have a powerful impact on our minds. When we experience romantic, familial or platonic love, our minds experience an increase in hormones including oxytocin and dopamine, which promote feelings of happiness, contentment and relaxation. Love also provides a sense of social support and connection, which contributes to improved mind health and a lower likelihood of depression or anxiety.

Additionally, the act of loving someone is beneficial for our minds. Showing love and kindness to others helps nurture our empathy, compassion and altruism, improving our mind health and strength. Focusing on the needs of others also takes the focus off our own problems and worries. This not only acts as a short-term distraction but also helps contextualise our worries and reduce our subjective experience of stress or anxiety.

NEUROTRANSMITTERS AND NEURORECEPTORS

Neurotransmitters and neuroreceptors are chemical messengers in our brains that work in a highly complex interplay. They are critical to the functioning of our minds and drive much of our behaviour. While understanding this incredible complexity is still the subject of much research, we do know that some of the most common neurotransmitters are serotonin, dopamine, endorphins, gamma-aminobutyric acid, glutamate, and noradrenaline. Each neurotransmitter has a unique set of functions, but they all work together and with neuroreceptors in complex and dynamic ways to influence our thoughts, emotions and behaviours. Different types of neurons have different neuroreceptors on their surfaces, which are specialised to respond to specific neurotransmitters.

Arguably, the most important neurotransmitters include serotonin, which regulates mood, appetite and sleep, and dopamine, which plays a key role in regulating reward, motivation and pleasure. In Chapter 1 we explored dopamine numbing and addiction, triggered by digital communication technologies that have proliferated and penetrated our minds in recent times. We can see the dangers of hijacking the dopamine reward mechanism in other activities that are more well known for their detrimental effect on our health, such as junk food, drugs, gambling and cults. We can also see this hijacking in a positive context. Consider the effect known as the 'runner's high' or 'endorphin rush', which describes the release of endorphins, our natural painkillers, when we exercise. In this way, the hijacking is working as a reinforcement motivator for an activity that is good for our health and strength. However, it is important, even here, to ensure awareness and balance since there are examples of exercise compulsion or even addiction that can have negative health outcomes.

Neuroreceptors are involved in a wide range of functions, including sensory perception, mood and behaviour. They also have a crucial role in processes such as muscle contraction and sensory perception and are involved in cell signalling. Imbalances in the neurotransmitter and neuroreceptor systems can lead to various mind health problems and reduce our mind strength, and even reduce our ability to build mind strength. It is, therefore, extremely important to keep our neurotransmitter and neuroreceptor systems healthy through high-quality and sufficient sleep, regular exercise, healthy nutrition and stress management.

EXERCISE AND NUTRITION

Physical exercise has a powerful effect on the mind, helping reduce symptoms of depression or anxiety and generally improving our mood.

It also seems to improve our cognitive functions, including memory, attention and neuroplasticity. Additionally, exercise enhances sleep quality and reduces stress by regulating our stress response systems.

The same benefits of regular physical exercise are also true of nutrition. The most important element of nutrition is water; our brains are 75% water, and even relatively low levels of dehydration significantly affect the mind. Drinking water is fundamental, but food can also be a significant source of water; for example, watermelon is 93% water.

Nutrients (vitamins and minerals) are important for mind health, as is a healthy gut microbiota. It is also vital to regulate blood sugar levels, as they directly affect our mind health and our cognitive functions.

EXERCISES

The following exercises can be thought of as 'mind hacks' and are especially useful to snap ourselves back to a more even keel, if we find our minds in a particularly high or low ebb. These mind hacks are not a replacement for overall mind health; they are complementary to the topics covered in the chapter and useful to support your development of mind strength. They are also particularly useful to help others you think may benefit from their effects, following the 'see one, do one, teach one' approach.

Relativise

Deeply consider how fortunate you are to live now in the context of all humans who have ever existed. You are almost certain to have the highest quality of life of any of your ancestors. Consider healthcare, heating, electricity and running water; these would have been unimaginable to even the most privileged. If you consider yourself compared to your direct line of ancestors, your reasons to be unhappy would likely pale into insignificance. This relativisation works further as you consider everyone else's ancestors and think about others across the world today.

Our ancestors endured significant challenges but were still able to live and reproduce. We have inherited their same minds, and so can imagine the pain and trauma they endured, whether that was living without shelter, heat, water, medicine or other critical resources. Our very existence proves our minds can withstand these extreme challenges. We should use the idea of our ancestors' extreme challenges to contextualise our own challenges. In fact, of all the challenges we could face, most of them have already been taken care of by our ancestors, and we continue to benefit from these innovations, systems and organisations every day. The modern world is luxurious for many people compared to the experience the vast majority of our ancestors endured, with most of our challenges addressed by our ancestors' solutions.

Actively comparing our full spectrum of challenges —including those that are largely solved, for example, heating, shelter, running water, etc. — to our worries is helpful for understanding their actual significance and not our subjective perception of their significance.

The list below highlights the recency of things we often take for granted today. Most of our ancestors lived before these things, which today many like to consider fundamental rights. Understanding how relatively fortunate we are should inspire your relativisation. We all have different motivators, so consider those that resonate most strongly with you:

- 1970s: central heating was first widely available
- 1940s: penicillin was first widely available
- 1919: only 6% of UK homes had electricity

- 1918 and 1928: right to vote in the UK for men and women, respectively
- 1900: first antibiotics
- 1840s: anaesthetics began to be used; prior to this, typically 80% of patients died of shock or infection
- 1830s–1840s: most people lived with no running water and faced unstoppable deadly epidemics like cholera, typhoid and influenza
- 1810: the hot shower was first invented, but was not widely available to the public until the 1920s in the US and the 1960s in the UK
- Pre-1800: very little effective medicine available beyond alcohol, opium and bloodletting with leeches

Third Person Yourself

To practise this exercise, choose a challenging situation you're currently facing. Step back and imagine you're observing yourself as a third person. Detach from your immediate mindset and visualise looking down on yourself from an outsider's perspective. Objectively observe the events unfolding, make a note of them and contemplate how you would expect another person to feel in the same context or situation. Reflect on the emotions and reactions that emerge during this exercise.

When considering how someone else would react, we usually conclude that our feelings are entirely justified and transient as the situation and context will inevitably pass. This is not a technique to remove ourselves from the situation but to provide insight, which confirms how we feel is justified objectively. However, most importantly, we gain insight that the feelings are not permanent but are the result of our context or situation. This insight bolsters our minds' strength and our confidence to battle on. Similar to the analogy of being in a storm while it is real and you are in the deluge, knowing that it will pass and that the sun will come out again gives you the strength to see it through.

Rip Tide

Imagine yourself caught in a rip tide and consider how your instincts and actions might differ when trying to fight it versus when you surrender and go with the flow:

- Contemplate the similarities between the rip tide situation and the challenges you are facing.
- Identify the aspects of your current situation that you can control and those that are beyond your control.
- Consider how shifting your focus to the controllable elements, and not worrying about the 'uncontrollables', can help you regain a sense of agency and reduce anxiety.

Practising Gratitude and Generosity

Express your gratefulness towards others regardless of the magnitude of their effort. Focusing on gratitude towards others involves intentionally recognising and appreciating the positive things that others do for us or their positive qualities.

The actual act of expressing gratitude can have numerous mind health benefits for the giver, including increased feelings of socialisation, improved relationships and reduced symptoms of depression and anxiety. In this way, expressing gratitude towards others helps foster positive emotions within us and deepens our connections with the people around us.

Try to make deliberate efforts to practise gratitude in your day-to-day routine. It can be the smallest of gestures or a more involved interaction. Ultimately, because it is such a simple and effective technique, it has a huge bang for its buck. It enables you to efficiently cultivate a sense of empathy, compassion and kindness, which will likely improve your, and others', mind health and strength. The impact of practising generosity is comparable to that of gratitude, impacting both your mind and the individuals you are generous to in similar ways.

Flip Anxiety to Excitement

Anxiety and excitement are experienced in our minds as fundamentally different emotions. However, they are, in fact, effectively the same from a physical and neurochemical perspective. Amazingly, this means we can quickly flip from anxiety to excitement by reframing our context or situation to a positive perspective. Both emotions trigger the release of adrenaline and noradrenaline, which ready the body for action. This increases heart rate, blood pressure and respiratory rate, leading to a sense of arousal and heightened awareness.

Experiment with doing this by thinking of something that you are anxious about and trying to change your perspective so you are excited by it. For example, consider an interview – you may be anxious because of the impact if you are not successful, or because you worry you may be found wanting. Now flip those feelings into excitement about the opportunity to explain your unique achievements, skills and experiences, meet some interesting peers and look back fondly on this moment in the future when you took the bull by the horns and were successful in the interview. By flipping your perspective or interpretation, your state of mind changes. That is, it changes from anxiety associated with an upcoming event to excitement through a positive interpretation. Self-awareness of this ability in our minds is hugely important as it allows us to improve our state of mind with a relatively small amount of effort. More importantly, having positive expectations can significantly influence outcomes. For instance, in the context of a job interview, being excited, in itself, is likely to yield better results than being anxious.

Universal View

Our minds are fully capable of the realisation and self-awareness of how small we are in the grand scheme of the universe. When we actively embrace this realisation, it is humbling and can help with our perspective and relativisation. When we actively consider the vastness of the cosmos and our place within it, we can relatively minimise the everyday worries or anxieties in our minds.

The James Webb telescope now allows us to see deeper into the universe than ever before, providing significant emphasis to the realisation of just how much we do not know and how much is undiscovered. Harnessing this awareness or realisation is a powerful tool in managing stress and anxiety since it helps us adopt a more open-minded and accepting perspective.

Try it yourself. Actively think about and embrace the realisation of the vastness of the cosmos and our existence within it. Now consider how your specific worries and anxieties feature within this universe. Embracing this relative perspective can help our minds more clearly recognise our relative place in the universe and more actively embrace the unknown; this can help us let go of the things that do not really matter.

Chapter 7.
Who Are the Other 8 Billion People?

Across the world our minds are overwhelmingly more similar than they are different. While there are clearly some differences, for example intelligence and the traits discussed in Chapter 2, across the 8 billion-plus of us on Earth these differences are relatively insignificant. One of our most consistent tendencies is the desire to belong to groups or tribes, and the lure of doing so. For our ancestors, this was critical for survival and the development of what we are today. While these tendencies remain of fundamental importance for driving positive outcomes, ironically, they are also frequently the root cause of significant negative outcomes too.

In this chapter we explore how the overwhelming similarity of our minds means any differences appear very stark, and our resulting fixation on these relatively tiny differences. We consider how our inherent draw to, and taking comfort in, a disproportionate focus on differences often causes us to actively ignore similarities and rely heavily on confirmation bias to inform our outlook. We start by examining the power of empathy, the significance of which cannot be overstated. Recognising that empathy has been touched on throughout this book, we'll consider here how it works and why it is so important.

EMPATHY

Empathy is an emotional ability to understand how others feel, and in some case even feel how they feel. It can be of no doubt that using empathy to understand how others feel was crucial for our ancestors' survival and continues to be fundamental in the current day for our societies to function. Harnessing and promoting empathy is hugely valuable for our mind health and strength; however, we also need to be aware of some potential pitfalls. Empathy is not without issues and can cause as many problems as the wonderful benefits it bestows on us, both individually and as groups. Empathy can be very subjective and cause us to unduly minimise rational or moral thoughts or behaviours. For example, we may ignore the overall benefits of an action because of a disproportionate influence of a highly emotional attachment.

It is generally understood that there are three main types of empathy: creative, emotional and existential. Creative empathy is putting yourself in someone else's shoes and imagining their experiences from their perspective as if you were them. Emotional empathy is closely associated with creative empathy and refers to feeling the same emotions as someone else, while existential empathy involves understanding the beliefs and values that shape another's mind.

Empathy is a critical component of a strong mind. When nurtured and cultivated, it is a superpower that enables our minds to build knowledge and navigate the world in a highly effective and rewarding manner. Practising empathy allows us to build deep, authentic relationships with others, form connections with other minds and gain a deeper understanding of the world around us. Empathy works by activating similar neural pathways to the person we are empathising with, which allows us to experience similar emotional responses.

Empathy is essential in creating knowledge in our minds, as it allows us to gain a more comprehensive understanding of different experiences and perspectives. Through empathising with others, we can learn from their experiences and integrate their insights into the creation of knowledge in our minds. This helps us to not only broaden our knowledge but also develop a broader, more inclusive and nuanced perspective.

A critical point to recognise as we cultivate empathy is that our minds do not all start from the same place. We have different life experiences and backgrounds, which directly shape our perspective. Practising empathy risks becoming less effective if we are not sincere in our desire to connect with and understand others' minds. This is why virtue signalling, as explored in Chapter 1, should be minimised, since it can often be suspected or deduced, even if this happens in our subconscious or is flagged by our intuition.

Empathy is a critical human capability and is responsible for much of our ancestors' success. However, the context in which our ancestors practised empathy is fundamentally different from the modern context, which means our approach to practising empathy must be different. Our ancestors likely engaged in empathetic behaviour with small, face-to-face groups. In today's world, the vast scale of suffering we encounter through the global interconnectedness powered by technology can quickly become overwhelming. Therefore, we need to be aware, as we are inundated with information, to manage our empathy on an individual level to ensure we are not overwhelmed, but are still able to offer empathy in a balanced way. While our subconscious minds perform much of this balancing act, we should seek to be actively aware when we are potentially not balanced in our empathy. For example, being too biased to a particular objective or cause because of a disproportionately impactful emotional trigger. This could be a love or hate based trigger that results in a lack of empathy and actions that wouldn't normally be aligned to your rational or moral sense. These types of emotional triggers can be particularly impactful when they result from deliberate, or unwitting, disengagement or ignorance.

The more we are aware of what our conscious and subconscious minds are doing in relation to empathy, the more we can ensure there are no unintended consequences corrupting our information flow and knowledge. We should also prioritise practising empathy as our ancestors did, seeking to do so face-to-face within small groups, to help us address the increasing isolation that is a feature of our modern context. This real-world contact activates our neurotransmitters instinctively and is crucial for mind health and strength.

GROUP AND TRIBAL INSTINCTS

We are instinctively drawn to groups and tribes, for good reasons that have enabled us, and continue to enable us, to survive, thrive and feel good (for example, though the dopamine reward system). However, they also cause us to be suspicious of outsiders and behave in a territorial manner, even when this is not in our group or individual interests. These instincts are encouraged and rewarded in every society, galvanising disparate groups of people around common goals. Arguments can be made for and against the merits of harnessing these instincts. For example, people feel good from having a sense of belonging to their favourite sports team, but this can also have negative impacts on the individual and others. Examples of potential negative impacts could include exploitation of the individual, or the results of religious persecution or sports-team-based hooliganism on others.

When we do embrace these group instincts, despite a clear wide range of benefits, there is a particularly noticeable negative side effect. This is the sense that all the 'other' people (i.e. those outside of our group) are fundamentally different and, worse still, often have nefarious intentions towards us. This side effect exists across the world, subconsciously or consciously, in almost every mind and is so powerful that our minds have developed pathways to convince us it is real. These pathways effectively dehumanise those we perceive as 'others' by projecting two fundamental ideas that 'prove' how different they are from us: firstly, how different their morality, values, empathy or even consciousness are compared to ours, and secondly, their inability to think, act in a planned manner and control themselves as we do. For each group of 'others', we assess how different they are based on these two ideas. This mechanism is often sufficiently convincing, such that we believe most of the other 8 billion people on Earth are somehow fundamentally different from us.

This inherent aspect of our minds does serve a purpose, and is even necessary in extreme cases – for example, shielding us from feeling all of humanity's pain. For example, if we were to feel empathy for everyone impacted by wars in the world today in the same way we do for our loved ones, it would be crippling. One of the ways we are able to compartmentalise this empathy is by convincing ourselves that 'they' are somehow different. While this can serve a purpose, it can also be very dangerous. Many tyrants and other nefarious actors have exploited this dynamic throughout history, and it could be argued it is a necessary prerequisite for any war. In the least pernicious form it has been, and continues to be, used to control and manipulate people. Because of the risks associated with this tendency, we should be actively aware of the groups we belong to and constantly challenge ourselves on how we think about people from other groups. We explored this previously in the section 'Team, Group, Tribes' in relation to our minds' craving for 'comfort foods'.

MORE SIMILAR THAN DIFFERENT

Since our minds are overwhelmingly similar, we tend to be fascinated by our differences. This fascination manifests as a completely disproportionate focus on relatively insignificant features of our minds. We should always seek to keep this awareness of our similarities as our primary framing of interactions with others. Similarities in the human mind exist across cultures in relation to traits and cognitive capabilities, and it is likely that individuals from completely different parts of the world with different ancestral backgrounds have very similar minds. In particular, the 'Big 5' personality traits (as explored in Chapter 2, Core Mind Strength) of openness, conscientiousness, extraversion, agreeableness and neuroticism are extremely consistent across cultures and languages, with little variation among different regions.[7] Additionally, cognitive abilities, such as working memory, attention and problem-solving skills, are largely universal and are not significantly affected by cultural context or background.

Therefore, we should ensure the relatively minor differences in our minds are not disproportionately the focus of all our attention. Active awareness of our innate urge to be fascinated by difference can help us instead focus proportionally more on what makes us similar. A good example of how this can manifest is recognising how our minds' fascination with differences is the root cause of creating stereotypes. While stereotypes would have been useful to our ancestors for rapid decision-making, they provide little value in our modern world, where we now understand that traits and intelligence are consistent across cultures and across the world. Stereotypes in our modern world only serve to obstruct effective communication and cause us to take actions that are not based on inaccurate premises or inferences.

Recognising how similar our minds are, rather than fixating on minor differences, brings into sharp focus the error of trying to group and segregate people, whether that is by race, gender, disability, personality, sexual orientation or anything else. These errors are born from, and amplified by, a lack of exposure to other minds. The experience of interacting with a diverse range of people quickly undermines the notion of different minds for different groups. In fact, ironically, similarities and opposites are significantly more likely to exist 'intergroup'. This means that there is significantly more chance of you finding a mind similar to yours in a completely different group, across the world's 8 billion people, than within your own group. The most important group we can belong to for our collective survival and thriving is the one that embraces our similarities at the expense of the group that does not.

EXERCISES

Exercise your mind by actively thinking about the 8 billion plus minds across the world and how they are significantly more similar than different. Consider the irony that this overwhelming similarity of our minds means we have become fixated on tiny differences and think about how we are able to maintain the illusion of major differences between our minds, for example through confirmation bias. Think about how empathy can be used to minimise or magnify these effects and the way you think about all the other people in the world. Create new neural pathways as you think through the questions, and experiment with the exercises and see which techniques work best for you:

- Explore in your mind – try it with your eyes closed or while doing physical exercise.

- Write down your thoughts, draw concepts or talk out loud to yourself.

- Work with others in dialogue.

Empathy

- Consider the definition of empathy and refresh your mind on the differences between the different types: creative, emotional and existential empathy:
    1. Think about their differences and similarities – are you more comfortable with one type over the other?
    2. Think about some examples of people you have had face-to-face interactions with, whether close friends or strangers:
        - Did they demonstrate any empathy for you?
        - What did it feel like for you, and how do you think they felt about being empathetic?
        - Do you think they benefited from it?
    3. Which types of empathy do you value, and how much of each do you want to receive from others?
    4. How much empathy do you currently practise, and which types do you feel most comfortable with?
    5. Do you want to be more empathetic in general or with a specific type of empathy, and what motivates this desire?
- Imagine yourself in someone else's shoes, considering a diverse range of people, whether real or imagined, historical or alive today, in similar or different contexts to yours:
    1. Try to really access your imagination to see things from within their mind and context to deeply understand their perspective.
    2. Reflect on how this exercise influences your thoughts and emotions about your own life.
- Consciously experiment with being more empathetic towards others:
    1. Practise trying to understand and share their emotions.
    2. Ask for feedback from these people on how they perceive your increased empathy.
    3. How does their response make you feel?

- Our ancestors would have practised emotional empathy within small groups face-to-face. Today, this type of empathy continues to have powerful healthy effects on our minds, and we should therefore strive to maintain interactions with family, friends, colleagues and strangers as an important part of our mind health.
- Consider existential empathy:
  1. How much do you appreciate others trying to understand your beliefs and values and how they shape your mind?
  2. What level of existential empathy really makes a difference to you?
  3. Do you think you could provide that level of existential empathy to others?

Groups

- Think of examples of groups that you see others in:
  1. What is the 'us versus them' dynamic?
  2. How strong is the belief that the members of the group are right and non-group members are wrong?
  3. What are the techniques the group uses to convince them that they are right, and the others are wrong?
  4. What are the benefits that the group draws from having these people in the group, and what does it demand from its members?
  5. Are there examples of groups where you see some in the group benefiting more than others?
  6. Are there examples where you see people being taken advantage of or exploited by their desire or need to be part of a group?
  7. Now, reflect on all these questions, but instead of groups you see others in, consider the groups you are in.

More Similar Than Different?

- Consider if you agree that the 8 billion of us on Earth are extremely similar. While thinking about this, consider a scenario where you happened to be born in a different geographic location or culture:
  1. Do you think you would have a fundamentally different mind?
  2. If you think you are overwhelmingly a product of your environment, what are the elements of your mind that are not from the context you were born and grew up in?
  3. What do you have in your mind that is not from your tribe? What is it and how did you get it?
- Think of examples where people put others in categories or groups, for example, by race, gender, disability, personality, sexual orientation or other abstract category:
  1. Are there any examples of this having bad outcomes?
  2. How much is this a result of people not having met enough people?
     - If they did meet enough people across all 'groups' they perceive in their minds, do you think they would see just as many similarities and differences as across any random selection of people?
  3. Consider the merits of grouping those who believe it is possible to group people versus those who do not – how important is ignorance in these groups?

To Wrap Up

Use what you have learned, the capabilities you have developed and the tools now at your disposal to robustly challenge this book. Consciousness is such a subjective qualitative experience, that it is likely there are topics covered in this book that you do not recognise from your own experiences, and no doubt things missing that you would consider crucial for mind strength. Scrutinise, interrogate, and vet these areas, both what is in the book and what is missing, using the insights and capabilities developed by a strong mind. Challenge yourself to develop exercises of your own to make your mind stronger across these areas. Actively avoid being dogmatic and always keep your mind open; the world is in shades, not absolutes, especially when it comes to making your mind strong.

Acknowledgements, Bibliography, Endnotes and Glossary
can be found at www.MindCallisthenics.com

Endnotes

1   Greg LeMond, Mark Hom (2014). "The Science of Fitness: Power, Performance, and Endurance", p.122, Academic Press

2   Dove Canada. (n.d.). The Dove Self-Esteem Project calls for action to address youth mental health crisis caused by social media. Cision. https://www.newswire.ca/news-releases/the-dove-self-esteem-project-calls-for-action-to-address-youth-mental-health-crisis-caused-by-social-media-885354751.html

3   Fardouly, J., Diedrichs, P. C., Vartanian, L. R., & Halliwell, E. (2015). Social comparisons on social media: The impact of Facebook on young women's body image concerns and mood. Body Image, 13(1), 38–45. https://doi.org/10.1016/j.bodyim.2014.12.002

4   Hinduja, S., & Patchin, J. W. (2010). Bullying, cyberbullying, and suicide. Archives of Suicide Research, 14(3), 206–221. https://doi.org/10.1080/13811118.2010.494133

5   Kruger, J., & Dunning, D. (1999). Unskilled and unaware of it: How difficulties in recognizing one's own incompetence lead to inflated self-assessments. Journal of Personality and Social Psychology, 77(6), 1121–1134. https://doi.org/10.1037//0022-3514.77.6.1121

6   Csikszentmihalyi, M. (2008). Flow: The Psychology of Optimal Experience. Ingram International Inc.

7   Hester, N., Xie, S.Y. and Hehman, E. (2021). Little between-region and between-country variance when people form impressions of others. Psychological Science, 32(12), 1907–1917. https://doi.org/10.1177/09567976211019950

Made in the USA
Monee, IL
07 July 2026

56552677R00089